I0659784

Is
The
Holy Ghost
Really
A Kerryman?

and other topics of interest

by

JOHN B. KEANE

THE MERCIER PRESS
CORK

THE MERCIER PRESS
Cork

© John B. Keane 1976

ISBN : 978-1-781-17893-5

For Miranda

Transferred to Digital Print-on-Demand in 2024

CONTENTS

IS THE HOLY GHOST REALLY A KERRYMAN?

Is the Holy Ghost really a Kerryman? The obvious answer to this is: If he is not a Kerryman what is he? Is he just another ghost, a mere figment of the imagination like Hamlet's father or Paul Singer's assets, or is he something more sinister; a Corkman masquerading as a Kerryman or worse still a real Kerryman but having an inferiority complex; that is to say a Kerryman who thinks he's only the same as everybody else?

I put it to you now that the question which I am about to pose is the one which holds the true answer. If the Holy Ghost is not a Kerryman can he be the Holy Ghost? The answer of course is no. He cannot. Having established his Kerryhood through theory we are at liberty to proceed so now let us establish it through logic. For this we need attestation, testimony. We need genuine witness. The following true story should be sufficient to dispel any remaining doubts concerning the real source of the spirit in question.

Some years ago one morning during the height of the month of June a young man set out from his home in the perimeter of a bustling city. He turned his face towards Kerry. He was fortunate enough to meet compassionate car drivers on his way so that between the jigs and the reels he found himself in the heel of the evening not far from that awe-inspiring terrain which is known in Kerry as The Conor Pass. In short he was nowhere else but in the seaside village of Castlegregory where the dispenser of his last lift had deposited him.

Here he betook himself to a hostelry where he partook of an egg and onion sandwich and three pints of well-conditioned Guinness's stout. At closing time-the barmaid asked him if he had acquired accommodation for the night but he replied that it was his intention to walk the lonesome road to Dingle, it being the month of June and he being in his health.

'But', said the barmaid who was young and beautiful and concerned, 'you'll have to climb all the ways to Conor Pass.' 'That', said the young man with a touch of bravado, 'is my exact intention.' So saying he buckled his knapsack, adjusted it on his shoulders and made for the open door.

'May the Holy Spirit guide you safe', said the barmaid. At this the young man scoffed and in that scoff was contained an implicit rejection of the power of the Holy Ghost. With a whistle on his lips the young man set off for the town of Dingle. Mile after mile of road he put behind him until the countryside started to fall away below him and he found himself at the entrance to Conor Pass, thousands of feet above the level of the sea. Here he slackened his pace for he felt that the worst part of his journey was over. Alas the mountains of Kerry are as unpredictable in temperament as the artists who paint them, the poets who so often extoll them and the playwrights who try to portray them.

Suddenly the mist began to thicken on the shoulders of the hills and in a matter of moments the young man couldn't see his hand in front of him. Blindly he groped his way along the narrow roadway knowing that one false step would plunge him into eternity. Inch by inch, foot by foot, he crawled along the road. Then without warning the ground began to slip away beneath his feet and he knew that he had strayed off the beaten path and that his life hung by a thread.

'Oh God', he shouted, 'Oh God help me.' There was nothing by way of reply but the sibilance of swirling mists and the whisper of growth deep in the vast tangle of mountain heather. He cried out again and again.

Then in answer to his summons a voice spoke. It spoke in

a whisper but it was a whisper of such intensity that it seemed as if all the winds of the world had assembled in that spot to enrich its timbre and deepen its volume.

'Tell me', said the voice in a Kerry accent, 'are you the man what don't believe in the Holy Ghost?'

The young man made no reply. The power of the mysterious voice had paralysed him. Then a huge and mighty hand, yet shapely, appeared out of the mist and taking one of the young man's hands it led him out of his impasse to where the stars danced in the midsummer sky and a white moon shone brightly on the lonesome road to Dingle.

Well now if that isn't sufficient testimony I don't know what is. From a purely personal standpoint I should inform you that I always invoke the aid of the Holy Spirit before embarking on any work of importance and if I were unexpectedly called upon tomorrow to write an epic poem on sardines or sausages I would journey first of all to Bally-bunion and thence to its seaweed baths where I would disrobe and submerge myself in the hot sea-water with fronds of glutinous seaweed enmeshing me in their slithery grasp. Then while the Atlantic raged outside I would uncork a bottle of Irish whiskey and indulge in a full-blooded hearty swallow. Up then in my pelt and off in a mad gallop towards the incoming tide. Then when I'm up to my neck in salt water I would invoke the Holy Ghost:

'Come to my aid oh great spirit. Infuse in me the white fire of minstrelsy.'

The moral, of course, in the aforementioned is that the poet who does not invoke his muse is a very foolish fellow.

* * * * *

THE CUCKOO

A few words about the cuckoo and the extraordinary effect he has on many of his listeners. God be with the days when every provincial newspaper carried reports of his arrival, when readers vied with each other in their claims of having been the first to hear him. Nowadays he is taken for granted the way everything else is. This is a shame because he has come all the way from Africa at his own expense to announce that summer is at hand. This is very important communication in this misty land of ours since we have few other assurances of summer's presence. We are indebted then to the cuckoo for making the arduous and perilous trip from Africa out of a sense of duty to those who are dependent upon his divulgements. For no material reward he abandons his sun-drenched habitat year after year to join with us in our awareness of summer.

Upon his arrival he looks for accommodation and on finding a nest to his taste he immediately evicts the tenants regardless of their age or sex. He sees no wrong in this coming as he does from a land which has only recently been introduced to the refinements of civilisation by dedicated remittance men, land-grabbers and second sons. He does not concern himself with the fate of the fledglings he has dispossessed. Rather he is content to survive within the circle of what naturalists refer to as the natural law. From a tourism point of view he would be perfectly entitled to the best possible accommodation on account of the favourable publicity he bestows so freely. He knows if he keeps cuckooing long enough that he will get other tourists to believe that the weather is delightful and not as bad as it would seem to be. Foodwise he fends for himself. His off-spring are fed by the parents of the former inmates of the nest so that he is no burden on the taxpayer. He provides his own transport which is of paramount importance in these days of unofficial strikes. He is rarely seen but always in the distance and in the obscurity of some leafy grove there is the heartening sound of his re-assuring pronounce-ments. He is the source of inspiration to hay-makers and turf-cutters. When they hear his dulcet voice they lift their heads and smile knowingly. They have just been notified that all is well with the world and that God is surely in His Heaven.

At this juncture my permanent retinue of carpers are sure to draw aside and take counsel. Why the cuckoo they will inevitably ask? Why this interloper from another continent not to mind another country?

What is he above the crow, the lark or the sparrow-hawk? He comes and he goes and he cuckoos in between or so it would seem to those who look no further than their noses. Ah my dear readers there is more to the cuckoo than mere cuckooing.

He is a landmark in the calendar of the year. He is as distinguished a visitor as the daffodil or the crocus or the hail that heralds the approach of winter. Socially he is the only truly communicative bird. Take your wild goose or duck. What have they to say for themselves beyond a squawk and a bashful clatter of wings when we surprise them in some arboreal retreat or sedgy shore. They eat more than the cuckoo and give nothing in return. Only for the rumbles from their bellies I doubt if they would know dinner hour from supper hour.

It is our bounden duty to make much of the cuckoo. We should at all times make note of his utterances and see to it that his arrival is made known to newspapers, neighbours and all other media who are willing to publicise his heart-raising revelations.

He has also contributed much to man's material needs. Poets and balladeers have made small fortunes out of him and often earned immortality for nothing else than extolling this remarkable tree-bird who asks so little in return.

He never fails to lift men out of their winter willies and look at the fortune he made for the man who first patented the cuckoo clock. Yet for all this he is shy and retiring and never imposes himself like magpies or sparrows. All I ask for is tolerance and a little respect for a creature whose outpourings are always associated with happy times and pleasant places. No man dare ignore the cuckoo with impunity and you may be sure that he who does not acknowledge the official voice of summer is not to be wholly trusted. You will find upon examination that he has other deficiencies but he who hails the wandering sprite and receives his disclosures with appropriate rapture is a man who knows the value of the finer things in life.

Yes dear readers it is our duty to pause and consider ourselves well blessed when first we hear his voice. It is time for rejoicing, for revelling and song for we have once again emerged from the darkness of winter and survived the harshness of spring. It will be a time to weep when his voice no longer assails us from grove and thicket, from spinney and copse. It will be the end of secret places and could well be the death-knell of those serene and shady places that exist in the back of beyond.

*   *   *   *   *

THE CONTAGEOUS CHOREA

There is an uncited disease, a mixture of hysteria, chorea and claustrophobia, which affects human beings collectively.

It leads to dangerous family rows and I am aware of cases where household implements have been used as weapons when the disease is at its most malignant. I once saw the mother of a decent home chase her youngest son with an aluminium kettle. Her intent was to strike him with the kettle and inflict a wound on his head.

On another occasion I saw the father of a household, as a rule a quiet inoffensive man, throw a large turnip at his sister who was, if anything, as quiet and inoffensive as her brother.

It should be explained that they were both short-term victims of this chorea I have mentioned and must not be held responsible.

The interested reader will ask if this disease is as common, for instance, as influenza or dandruff. It is, but it is more carefully concealed. In fact some families are ashamed to admit that they have endured bouts of it.

It is commonest in large families and its chief cause is exhaustion. It begins suddenly over nothing and later when deranged households endeavour to discuss how it all started there is not a whit of evidence to aid them in their investigations.

You may search medical textbooks till you are old and grey but nowhere will you find a reference to contagious chorea. You will come across countless examples of mass hysteria but this is not quite the same thing.

Contagious chorea is, I believe, the annual spring-cleaning

of the mind. Injustices are exposed and evaluated, accusations are levelled and stout defences put forward. Minor infringements of the household code come under the spotlight and there follows a witch hunt of Salem-like proportions.

In the beginning there is peace and quiet. The father may be sitting reading his newspaper, the mother knitting contentedly, the younger children watching television, the older children getting ready to go to a dance and so forth and so on. Suddenly one of the youngsters hits his brother or sister a wallop and retaliation follows. This happens often enough and that's the end of it but on this occasion there is a chain reaction. All the children start hitting one another. Father and mother rise to assume control. The mother's knitting gets caught in the father's legs and the father shouts: 'Is there no peace to be got in this house?' This comment is addressed to no one in particular but the wife knows full well that she is being held responsible.

'Why don't you leave', she shouts, 'if it doesn't suit you!'

This is unfair and the father knows it. He cannot leave, even if he wanted to. He walks out of the room, slamming the door, and outside collides with his eldest daughter who is carrying her dance frock delicately to her room. The dance frock suffers from the collision but there is no apology from the father. The chorea spreads and the daughter dances on the dress. She abandons the dress and enters the room the father has just vacated. She bangs the door to give vent to her fury.

'Stop banging that door!' says the mother.

'What a place to live!' says the daughter.

The mother draws a clout at her and, in turn, the older daughter hits one of the children. Now, everyone, everywhere in the house, is at it. The father catches one of his sons about to don one of his ties. Normally he would not say a word but now he kicks the son on the behind and threatens him with expulsion should he every catch him with a tie of his again. The son goes into a bedroom, not forgetting to bang the door. All over the unhappy home doors are banging and the sounds of discord are spreading. Nobody is safe. One member of the family who is sick in bed is told to get out of it and quit the shamming. A sick man who is half asleep is as dangerous as a wounded water-buffalo and must never be provoked. He rises from the bed in his pyjamas and goes around seeking whom he may devour. He finds his father leathering one of the children and accuses him of unnecessary brutality. The father departs in a rage and the sick man takes up the leathering where the father left off. Now nobody is safe and there is nowhere to hide. Yet nobody vacates the premises. It is as if they know that this storm must be endured. A family is as strong as its weakest link and if one seeks refuge outside the chain he betrays his breeding and his instincts.

Now the tide of battle sways back and forth uncertainly. There are screams and yells. Doors bang with the frequency of machine gunfire and a pane of glass is heard breaking. Somebody hurls a dinner plate at a fireplace and children hide in crannies to escape the wrath of their elders.

Then, suddenly, beautifully, mercifully, the storm ceases and the sounds of clangour fade completely. The family has successfully withstood the test. All is well and the house abounds with the sounds of contrition and love. Nobody knows how it began and nobody cares. The important thing is that it's over, that all feelings have been relieved, all frustrations annihilated. Everybody is kind to everybody else and then, unexpectedly, someone starts to laugh and soon the house is rocking and rolling with irrepressible and contagious laughter.

LONG-DISTANCE TALKERS

I once knew an actor who always included a few lines of his own whenever he got on the stage.

He couldn't help it. He was a natural talker. It was always necessary to tie a piece of fishing gut on to his trousers and to chuck it hard two or three times to remind him that it was time to give somebody else a chance.

Talking is a God-given gift and an incomparable means of communication. We often heard it said of a woman that she was a terrible talker. This does not mean that she was a nagger. Yapper would be a more descriptive word. This woman's husband generally has to wait a long time for his dinner. He doesn't complain because he knows she can't really help it. He knows she is standing at some corner with her shopping-bag in her hand bemoaning the state of the world with a colleague of the same bent. He knew before he married her that she was an incurable talker and this was one of the reasons why he pursued her. He liked to hear her chattering aimlessly about inconsequential things and her talk held a music for him that was to be found in no other. Her neighbours might say of her: 'God bless her, she'd talk the hind leg off a pot!' but for him the ceaseless murmur of her voice was a source of the greatest joy.

I have heard certain women referred to as talking machines. These can talk for any given length of time on any subject from any position you care to name. They can screw their heads around in buses and deliver marathon speeches to friends several seats away. They can lean out of upstairs windows at unbelievable angles and talk about neighbours or malt and cod liver oil. They can outline the progress of Ecumenical Councils and debate the outcome of unpredictable romances. They live for talk and it is a strange fact that these women are married to men who prefer not to talk at all.

A truly talkative woman will talk under any circumstances. She will talk where it is forbidden to talk but I believe that no woman should be restrained. I like talkative women. I like to listen to them and to savour the cadences and pitches of their women's voices. Often, in buses and trains, I have closed my eyes and listened while a woman's voice introduced me to unknown worlds of hats and blouses and shoes and I have convinced myself that there is a lot to be learned from listening regardless of the subject under discussion. I can close my eyes and hear of confirmation dresses and party frocks of yellow organdy. Sometimes, if I'm lucky, I hear incredible descriptions of model husbands and even though I know there isn't an ounce of truth in them my heart is on the side of the woman who paints a rosy, if untrue, picture of her own beloved partner.

There are some other talkers whom I don't like. They are peculiar to trains and buses. They introduce themselves to total strangers and keep up an irritating flow until the victim is obliged to depart his seat or compelled to tell the intruder to shut up and go away. It is no use pretending to be asleep because the sworn talker is generally contaminated with a voice like a rasp.

I cannot stand loud and obstreperous talkers, or if you like, aggressive talkers. These are usually to be found in public houses and they generally manage to unsettle the composure of peaceable drinkers so that the pub is no longer a place of retreat. But an old gentleman who owned a country pub was master of occasions like these. He was the possessor of an old gramophone which he turned on whenever a vainglorious and fight-seeking shouter got out of hand.

There are other quieter types who like to talk to themselves. I often talk to myself, sometimes contentedly and other times contentiously. There's many a man who likes to praise himself and on the other hand to deride himself, because there is nobody sufficiently interested in him to care whether he deserves praise or blame for his way of living. Some types talk to themselves all the time even when they are being addressed by others. There was an old man I knew who talked to himself all the time. He was asked one day by a curious young fellow why he persisted in talking to himself all the while. 'Because I never met a nicer fellow than myself,' the old man replied.

Sometimes after rows in the home and outside it, the protagonists do not talk to each other at all for long periods. In the home this is a good thing because it frequently provides a breathing space or lull which is very necessary where people are eternally conscious of each other. Outside the home it is foolish and cruel and it is always painful to hear of people who do not talk to each other. It is misusing the power of speech and it is a root cause of indigestion and neuralgia. It passes from one generation to another and, in time, although the breach is not healed, a man forgets his reasons for not talking to another man, so if there's someone to whom you're not talking, put it off no longer. Bid him the time of day the next time you meet and as sure as there's meat on the shin of a wren, it won't be long before the pair of you will be talking.

*　*　*　*　*

PIPE DOWN PLEASE

I have written on numerous occasions about pipes. These include tobacco pipes, drainpipes and bagpipes to mention but a few but I honestly feel that I have never devoted enough time or study to tobacco pipes. Daily I become more convinced of this when I see growing numbers of people who have no qualification at all or no right to go around with pipes in their mouths. Many people carry pipes in their mouths whose heads, jaws and teeth were never designed for such a purpose. They rarely smoke the pipes. The carry them purely for effect or to give the impression that they know a lot more than they are prepared to divulge. Another conclusion I have drawn is this. When a man has nothing to say, as for instance when he is badly beaten in debate, his clenched teeth are fit for nothing else but the holding of a pipe. In effect it could be said that he is hiding behind his pipe.

For a while after I gave up cigarettes I apprenticed myself to pipe-smoking. I could make no fist of it so one day while watching a local football final I took my pipe from my mouth and flung it in disgust in the general direction of the referee.

Since then I have left pipes to those who know how to smoke them. However, let us now list, for the benefit of the student, some of the many ways in which pipes are misused by those who smoke them and those who pretend to smoke them. If I overlook some of the more glaring misuses it is because I am by nature a soft-hearted and well-meaning chronicler who wishes ill-will to no one and who would not like to make a show, as it were, of certain guilty parties in front of their wives and families.

There is in every community a man, sometimes more than one, who lives in perpetual fear of being assaulted. There may be good reason for his fear but, whatever the cause, he believes that footpads, thugs and others of evil intent are waiting for him behind every telephone pole, in every open doorway, around every corner and even under the bed in his own home. This is the sort of innate fear that breeds its own particular defence mechanism. So what does our friend do? He buys a pipe and every time he ventures out of doors he places the pipe firmly between his teeth. The idea is to suggest, through his bared fangs, that he is not to be molested. It does not matter if the smoke gets in his eyes or if his tongue is a mass of blisters from the excessive drawing.

His likely enemies are wary of him while he has the pipe in his gob. His lips are drawn back from the two rows of clenched molars and there is a snarly look about him that is almost wolfish in its ferocity.

At heart he is as windy as an overblown balloon but lesser men get out of his way as he strides through the streets with tobacco smoke billowing behind him. The problem here is that, sooner or later, he will foolishly believe that he is as tough as he looks and risk a collision with a man who is either too shortsighted or too stubborn to get out of his way. A man with a pipe in his mouth is easy meat in a clash of bodies. The pipe automatically leaves the mouth at the moment of impact and as a result our friend is without his armour for the rest of his journey.

Let us now look at the man who taps his pipe against the heel of his shoe. A man who does this is one of two things. He is an incompetent and daring bluffer or a very proficient fellow indeed. Since there is and always has been a woeful deficiency of very proficient men in this world we may safely presume that the vast majority of those who tap the bowls of their pipes against the heels of their shoes are inefficient, incompetent and always late for appointments.

18

The tapping against the heel is to imply efficiency, to suggest to onlookers that the heel-tapper is a practised pipe-user who has forgotten more about the art of pipe-smoking and pipe-handling than most ever learn and that because he is practised at one thing it should follow as the night the day that he is practised at everything.

Your heel-tapping pipe-smoker fools nobody and in the long run all he has to show for his gameze is a broken pipe.

Let us now press on to a very rare type indeed. This is he who continually carries a pipe in his hand but never puts it in his mouth. Just when it seems certain that he is about to place it between his teeth he withholds it and waves it in one direction or another to indicate a point in time or a place in distance. He may even use it to stress an aspect of his argument or often he may use it as a pointer for maps, charts and points of the compass.

The case I would like to make is that he will use it for anything but smoking and this in the last analysis is the greatest misuse of all.

Before I close let me parade another type before the reader. This man walks abroad with a pipe in his mouth and with his head in the air. Yet he is neither fearful nor alert for attack. He is just another proud man with new false teeth and he is using his pipe to exhibit them in public for the first time.

*   *   *   *   *

WAKES

Now we will deal with wakes, funerals, graveyards and things of such a nature. Do not hasten away I beg of you. There is a lighter side to everything.

One of my favourite pursuits is strolling through churchyards. It is a recently-acquired pastime and it comes, I have no doubt, from a subconscious necessity to familiarise oneself with the sort of location where one will be forced to reside until Gabriel sounds his horn on the last of all days. There is, of course, the fact that there are few places more peaceful but I prefer to believe that it comes from this submerged need to identify with the last resting place.

I used also like to attend wakes where the accent was on relief rather than grief, that is to say wakes of a cheerful nature where the departed person would have been a mighty age or might have suffered overlong from some awful disease. This sort of wake was an occasion for rejoicing rather than grieving and if the aged party had left behind a modest portion of worldly goods then there was more reason than ever for celebration.

However, an outward appearance of sorrow had to be maintained. It was expected of the next-of-kin and although the deceased might have been no loss he was at least entitled to sad and sober visages from those of his relations who had been left behind for reasons which are never stated by the Party responsible. We can only surmise that He knows what He is doing.

When I was a gorsoon there was a good deal of protocol to be observed when the wakehouse was entered. First of all one shook hands with every member of the household.

If you were a woman you were expected to embrace and kiss the female members of the household.

Then one knelt to pray in the room where the corpse was laid out. Seated in this room would be several local women who always maintained serious and even cross faces lest some drunken intruder misbehave in the presence of the dead person. Some of these, the more intimidating, would be well-positioned at the head of the bed from where every visitor would be visible. Sometimes they would engage in whispered conversations but only when they wished to enquire about the identity of some strange mourner who might not have been seen in the district before. These doughty women were very necessary when the pubs closed and when every type of blackguard was let loose on the countryside in search of diversion. They were the vigilantes of the dead.

The wake-room was an ominous place where one first briefly examined the corpse and his manner of dress. Then one knelt down at the side of the bed, bent one's head and subscribed a decent number of prayers towards the heavenly welfare of the dead person. Then one rose slowly and exited to where the drink was. People with special claims would squeeze the dead man's hand or bend over the bed and kiss his brow. In the kitchen or the 'Room' which were the areas where the drink was in fullest circulation one ten dered still more sympathy to whosoever might be in charge of the drink. I remember once being present at the wake of an elderly man who had succumbed to an unexpected heart attack having returned home from his first holiday abroad. The gentleman in whose company I happened to be was a great man for protocol and after we had said our prayers in the wake-room we proceeded leisurely to the drinking room. Here he shook hands with a woman who was handing out mugs of porter to all and sundry. He waited till she was about to dip an empty mug into the sudsy surface before he tendered his summation:

'God bless us and save us', said he to the woman, 'but he's as handsome a corpse as ever I seen in my life.'

'He's all that', said she, 'but of course the fortnight's holiday done him the world of good.'

Because of this astute comment we were handed glasses of whiskey so that our stomachs would have the requisite bases for the large draughts of porter which were sure to follow. We drank several mugs of the nourishing stuff and at the hour of midnight a Rosary was said. After that the older and the more sensible of the mourners betook themselves to their own homes. Stories were then told, humourous and bawdy and maybe a bar of a song in a low key. I remember a story I once heard at the waking of a relation in the Stacks' Mountains.

There was an old man in his nineties who had been married for nigh on fifty years. One night in his sleep he gave up the ghost but instead of sending for the priest and doctor his old woman decided to leave him in the bed for a while longer, for seven days to be exact. At the end of that time she roused a neighbour and told him that her husband was dead. She asked him if he would be good enough to go for the priest and doctor.

'I will to be sure', said he, 'and when will I tell them he died?'

'A week today', said the old woman.

'And why didn't you come for me before this?' said the neighbour.

'Well', said the old woman, 'we always promised each other we'd have one quiet week together.'

In my youth too a wake was a great place to settle a family quarrel. It was the ideal time for such conflagrations. Drink was abundant and nerves were stretched taut for want of sleep. No great notice was taken of those outbursts. It was only when the porter ran out that cnamhshawling was to be heard. There are very few wakes these days for the good reason that most people now die in hospitals and there are countless other diversions such as television and bingo.

EPITAPHS

Here lie the bones of Pecos Bill,
He always lied
And always will.
He once lied loud
He now lies still.

The above was one of the first epitaphs I ever learned. I heard it on the stage of the Plaza Cinema in Listowel from the lips of a strolling player when I was ten years of age and ever since I have had a hunger for epitaphs of a comic nature. The first original epitaph I ever heard was composed by a local poet named Paddy Drury:

Here lie the bones of Paddy Drury
Owing their size to Guinness's Brewery.

It was never to appear on his headstone which was recently erected at the Old Abbey of Knockanure near Listowel. The reverend mother of the home in Killarney where he died begged him not to allow it to be used so he acceded to her request. My personal choice in epitaphs is that which was devoted to a hanged sheep-stealer named Thomas Kemp:

Here lies the body of Thomas Kemp
Who lived by wool and died by hemp.

In second place comes:

Here lies my wife,
In earthy mould
Who when she lived
Did nought but scold.
Good friends go softly
In your walking

23

Lest she should wake
And rise up talking.

For my own epitaph I would not be too choosy. Something simple and catchy like the following:

Here lie the bones of John B. Keane.
I hope the grass above is green.
And when the summer comes around
May daisies dance upon this ground.

Nothing pretentious. Whatever about the hereafter the most one can hope for in the clay is grass and a daisy or two and, of course, a prayer now and then. I rarely pass by a graveyard if I see one from the roadway but while Ireland abounds in graveyards, quaint, elegant and otherwise the same cannot be said for epitaphs. For such a colourful and humorous people we are notoriously shy when it comes to inscribing our headstones and tombs with writing that is memorable. This is why so few people visit Irish graveyards. In England thousands of visitors call each year to graveyards which have comic inscriptions on their headstones.

There is one honorable exception to the Irish position and that is the churchyard of Kilfergus in the town of Glin in County Limerick. Here is an outstanding example:

Erected to the memory of Thos. Pope Hodnett, died Dec. 26th, 1847. They say he was an honest man. Erected by his son Thos. Hodnett, Pastor, Immaculate Conception Church, Chicago.

In the same graveyard which is ever open to passers-by there is perhaps the best-penned epitaph in the country. When I last saw it less than a month ago the characters were as clear as could be on the stone.

Erected to the memory of Timothy Costello, died June 4th, 1873:

This is the grave of Timothy Costello
Who lived and died a right good fellow.

From his boyhood to life's end
He was the poor man's faithful friend.
He fawned before no purse-proud clod.
He feared none but the living God.
And never did he do to other
But what was right to do to brother.
He loved green Ireland's mountains bold,
Her verdant vales and abbeys old.
He loved her music, song and story
And wept for her long-blighted glory.
And often did I hear him pray
That God would end her spoilers' sway.
To men like him may peace be given
In this world and in Heaven.

*   *   *   *   *

FARMERS' BOYS

This essay constitutes a farewell to farmers' boys. It does not propose to look at the whole history of the farmer's boy as distinct from the 'Spailpín' or seasonal worker. It will examine some aspects of his existence before he was designated an agricultural worker by a more benign form of government than that which existed during the days of the hiring fairs and Spotting Days.

Your true farmer's boy was a part-time poet as well as being a part-time cobbler, tailor and barber. Depending on your point of view he was as odious to his detractors as Free State Soldiers, Republicans, Blueshirts and Emergency Men were to theirs. He was very often blamed for disorders in which he hadn't hand, act or part but this could be because men of property were fond of blaming all kinds of civil strife on men who had no property. It is also a known fact that when men of no property aspire to property they quickly shed their socialistic tendencies. The farmer's boy is the only livelihood with which I am acquainted which offered no promotion or material advancement to those who opted for it or were forced into it as a career.

The hours were long and the pay was small. Worse still supply exceeded demand and innocent labourers who dared mention the world 'union' in those benighted days were regarded as out-and-out anarchists with nothing else in their heads but the ultimate destruction of church and state. District justices upon hearing that the defendant before them was a farmer's boy would lift their heads and peer hard and long at the unfortunate creature whose only crime might be that he temporarily purloined a bicycle from some street corner in the town lest he be late for the milking of the cows in the morning. I once heard a conservative politician on the eve of a general election make the following remark:

'This country', said he, 'is full of farmers' boys and low-down latchikoes that has to be kept in their proper place. Jail isn't good enough for them', he went on, 'but if we gets in we'll work them to the marrow of the bone.' No wonder the emigrant ships were full.

I remember a court case at which I was a spectator. In my youth I was fond of spending long periods in court. It was a good way to pass the time and there was always the promise of drama. One afternoon the case in question was called. A farmer's boy was suing his employer for extra wages for the simple reason that the food promised by the farmer in the original agreement between the two had not been forthcoming. When the farmer's boy's name was called out the judge quipped; 'bring him up so that we can have a look at him.'

The farmer's boy whose name was Tom entered the dock where he was examined closely by the justice who peered out over his spectacles in a most inquisatorial manner.

'You look a hardy fellow', said the judge.

'Oh he's a prime buck your honour', said the solicitor who was defending the farmer. The solicitor for the farmer's boy objected strenuously and cited grievances for his client. The chief of these was that the farmer had promised three square meals a day, the midday meal being the chief one to consist of bacon and cabbage or as was more commonly known, mate and cabbage. The farmer swore on oath that his wife had always given the boy mate and cabbage enough.

'Yes', interjected the boy, 'mate and cabbage enough but never cabbage and mate enough.'

It was a good point but in the justice's view enough was enough be it cabbage and mate or mate and cabbage.

The case was lost. I'll concede that there were instances

when your farmer's boy was not above setting fire to a hay-stack rather than take his grievances into court. These were honest hard-working men, underpaid and underfed. How true the old Latin quotation: *Probitas laudatur et alget* which means in English: 'Honesty is praised and starves.'

References were never asked of a farmer's boy. If he was big and strong, prepared to work long hours, seven days in the week, to draw back from the table early and not be looking for tasty diet this was the best possible reference. As I said earlier they were also part-time poets and they often rhymed out of pure hunger. Take the case of the farmer who presented the four men he had working for him with fat, lardy bacon for dinner. One composed the following on the spot:

> Oh Lord on high who rules the sky
> Look down upon us four
> And give us mate that we can ate
> And take away the boar.

* * * * *

PUDDING-FILLING

Many readers will remember my many deeply-researched treatises on the subject of pudding-bending. It could be said that we presented a complete picture and eventually deduced that pudding-bending was as high an art as any. High, however, as we made it out to be there is a kindred art which far excels it and it is with this art that I now propose to deal. Let us then take a look at the art of pudding-filling by hand or, if you like, the history of home-filled puddings.

At the time of writing I know only three female pudding-fillers. Time was when I knew a hundred or more. This was when every house in the countryside fattened its own pig and cured its own bacon. You can have smoke without fire and love without music but you cannot, no matter what, have home-filled puddings without pigs.

Having established this we may proceed. Your greater, grey-haired female, pudding-filler was a very formidable figure indeed. Today's pudding-filler is a gentler more easy-going type but this could well be because she has less to contend with.

Your matriarchal pudding-filler would collect her own blood. That is to say she would hold the basin under the pig's throat when that same throat was unceremoniously gartered by the local pig-butcher. Sometimes there was disaster, subsequent to which there would be panic and still subsequent to which there would be a loss of blood from the blood bowl as well as the pig. The greater the blood loss from the bowl the smaller the number of puddings. The smaller the number of puddings the likelier the prospect of making enemies since there would have to be a reduction in the normal quotas for neighbours and friends. Hyper-sensitive neighbours, always on the alert for signs of disrespect and slights, are too hasty to misread the significance of reduced quotas. They presume that other less-deserving neighbours have received more and are not above returning their meagre allocations on the grounds that they are being discriminated against. It is, therefore, wiser to appoint a member of the family or a close friend to a job in public relations before the actual distribution is made. This person might intimate that blood had been lost or that because of a small or anaemic pig there was likely to be a reduction in the over-all number of puddings for distribution. In short he would convey that nobody would be deliberately wronged.

Odd as it may seem it must be recounted that offence is never taken if the amount of porksteak is minimal. It is solely by the size and number of puddings that the recipient evaluates his importance in the eyes of the giver.

As soon as the blood has been gathered the pig is opened down the middle and the guts are removed. These are steeped and cleaned for it is into these guts that the mixture of blood is stirred repeatedly and salted lest it coagulate. Then a pound or so of good quality beef suet is chopped and added as are the chopped bodies of several respectable onions. Then comes the spice and the pepper and the oatmeal, pin-head if at all possible. The mixture is stirred repeatedly and allowed to rest for several hours when it is finally stuffed into the cleaned-out guts. There are some pudding-fillers who chop up the pig's liver and add it to the mixture. It is purely a matter of taste.

A funnel is used to convey the rich mixture into the guts and a piece of wood is used as a ramrod. In this way pudding after pudding is filled and when there is a potful tiered and ready they are boiled. Some women like to boil the puddings a second time as they insist it results in a firmer pudding which will not go to pieces in the frying pan but others hold that if the puddings are filled properly in the first place one thorough boiling is more than adequate. Having eaten single and double boilings on numerous occasions I must say that I personally favour the single boilings and I am of the belief that the second boiling knocks a lot of the good out of the puddings. Other eminent authorities hold with me in this.

As the mixture dwindles from the incessant filling a serious problem often arises. This is that there are too many guts and too little filling. Some women fill on regardless and dump the left-over guts. Others, however, dilute the mixture with cold tea or water and add breadcrumbs, chopped onions, oatmeal and chopped suet. The ultimate products are known as second-run-puddings. Naturally they lack the texture of the first-run but they are considered ideal for poor relations, old folk, townspeople, children etc.

The porksteak and puddings are then made up into neat parcels and for special friends a few spare-ribs are thrown in for good measure. I hope I have been of some assistance to prospective pudding-fillers and I would like to remind them when they are making out their lists that I too have a tooth for a well-filled pudding.

*   *   *   *   *

TRACING RELATIONS

Being reared in the countryside has many advantages. You get to know people better and people get to know you. The countryside is different from the city in many ways but the most significant difference is that, in the country, every man has status whereas in the city men tend to submerge their identities and often lose them altogether.

In the country a man, no matter what his calling may be, is subject to considerable scrutiny when his name comes up. The name may have appeared in a local paper for having defective headlamps or bald tyres or for involvement in a fracas outside a dancehall or a chip-shop in the nearest town. He may have merited inclusion for the scoring of a last-minute point in a junior football engagement or his name may have cropped up for some reason not worth a mention in the newspapers.

It could well be that he hails from a place several miles distant but is in the process of charming a local girl with a view to marriage. Because his name is not locally known he is bound to be the subject of much curiosity and this curiosity is nearly always satisfied by the wide knowledge of a wise local who might be called a Tracer. A Tracer is one who can trace relations to the fourth, fifth and sixth connections and provide a person with the history of rural families who have been mysteriously ignored by publications like *Who's Who?*, *Burke's Peerage* and *Landed Gentry* to mention but a few.

Let us illustrate by example. When I was a gorsoon roaming the Stacks' Mountains I was in the habit of calling to a house where dwelt one of the most distinguished Tracers in the entire countryside. His name was Jer Orchard and he was so called because two frustrated apple trees stood at either side of his humble abode. Jer was much in demand by postmen, insurance agents, guards and pensions' officers. These would be town-based for the most part and, therefore, would have a poor knowledge of the countryside and its people. I remember well a March morning when Jer Orchard's talent as a Tracer was put to its severest test. We were sitting by the fire at the time discussing the weather and the price of cattle when unexpectedly the latch was lifted and in came the postman. He had no letter for Jer Orchard or for Jer's son or daughter-in-law or for any Orchard whomsoever.

There were beads of perspiration on his brow and his hands hung limply by his sides.

'I'm killed stone dead,' said he, 'looking for the house of F. X. Maldowney.'

'What's the address?' Jer Orchard asked without taking the pipe from his mouth. This was no more than a routine question for a man of Jer's immense knowledge.

'All there is,' said the postman holding the letter aloft, 'is F. X. Maldowney, Lyre, Co. Kerry.'

Jer Orchard repeated name and address over and over again. The more he repeated the information the more puzzled he sounded.

'You're better be wetting a mouthful of tay,' he said to the daughter-in-law.

'There are three hundred Maldowneys in this postal district,' said the postman, 'and F. X. could be any one of them.'

The tea was duly drank and after he had returned to his seat by the fire Jer Orchard commenced his cogitation once more.

'If it beats you,' said the postman, 'I'll have to try all the Maldowneys and that will take from here till Doomsday.'

'Contain yourself,' said Jer Orchard calmly and again he

33

took to repeating the name and address; F. X. Maldowney, Lyre, Co. Kerry. He ruminated for several minutes and then he took the pipe from his mouth.

'Blasht me,' said he, ''tis no one but Fredeen Plant.'

'I declare to God,' said the postman, 'but you're as right as the rain.'

Let us now look at Jer Orchard's method of identifying Fredeen Plant. The name F. X. stood for Frederick Xavier Maldowney near whose farmhouse stood a small plantation of Sitka spruce. The day Frederick-Xavier Maldowney planted the Sitkas he was immediately christened Frederick Plantation and eventually because the trees were somewhat stunted Fredeen Plant.

All the people of the area with the honourable exception of Jer Orchard had forgotten that under the nondescript label of Fredeen Plant was concealed the luxurious title of Frederick Xavier Maldowney.

*   *   *   *   *

LOSING ONE'S WAY

I have lost count of the number of times I have been stopped in the streets of Dublin by people who have lost their way. When I answer that I am a stranger to the place myself they look at me as if I were to blame for their misfortune. I would dearly love to help these people and send them on their proper roads but I am not omniscient and I am prepared to lay odds that I have been lost more often than they. I can sympathise with them when their questions bear no fruit because I have asked these questions countless times myself and I know the resultant feelings of frustration.

In the early days when ordinary passers-by would explain that they were unfamiliar with the places I desired to visit I would always wait until I saw a member of the Garda Siochana. I discovered that most of the Garda Siochana one met on the streets of Dublin were as familiar with the city as I was myself. That is to say they merely knew the basics such as the way to Kingsbridge or Amiens Street and even a short cut to the Pillar but if you asked them where was Mooneys of White's Lane where they sold the clay pipes there would be the familiar lifting of the cap and the inevitable scratching of the head. The best bet was to bide one's time and inspect convenient shop windows until an old woman with a handbag happened to come the way.

I discovered after years of trial and error that elderly women with handbags knew their immediate vicinities like the backs of their hands.

There are many reasons for this. Old women in cities seldom wander far from their own doorsteps, preferring the small neighbourhood shops to the bewildering mazes known as supermarkets in the busy areas of the city. There is another reason. They no longer possess the confidence to mount buses or cross busy intersections. Frail and uncertain they cling to quieter streets within a short radius of their abodes. They listen patiently when asked a question and sometimes due to faulty hearing will ask for a repeat. They take their time and ponder well the name of a shop or the street in question. With a sad shake of the head they will sometimes tell you that it is not there anymore. I well remember asking an old lady who carried a handbag if she knew the whereabouts of a typewriter-repair shop which I had visited many years before but had forgotten the precise situation in the meanwhile. She shook her head to indicate that I had posed her a tough one but at the same time I could see that she relished a challenge, that it was a test for her failing memory.

'Ah yes,' she said, 'that would be little Mister Lollery.'

'That was the name of the man,' I said.

'The Lord be good to him,' she said and she made the sign of the cross. Then changing her bag from one hand to the other she launched into an account of his death and decline. When he found he wasn't feeling well he sold the goodwill of the shop to a tailor who now had a flourishing business but who hadn't half the heart of Mister Lollery who'd give you the shirt off his back. Before we parted company she told me that he had gone to live with his daughter for awhile but after a few months he got 'what I hope you'll never get sir' which meant some malignancy like cancer against which there was no defence. She was right about Mister Lollery. On the one occasion I did business with him I found him to be a decent oul' skin who looked downright apologetic when he had to take a few bob.

Another good source of directions is your postman, that's if you're lucky enough to catch one. Then there are publicans. Publicans and their assistants, while they may not know the place themselves, will always find somebody who does. Most people, however, you meet on city streets just haven't a clue so that it's no use fuming or losing one's temper when after a long period of probing and counter probing one is as near to one's destination as one was in the beginning.

In the country where everybody knows everybody else it's much easier and there is little likelihood of losing one's way for long. When you meet a fool treat him like a fool, that is with respect and courtesy, two commodities incidentally for which fools always long. When you meet a smart alec treat him like a smart alec, with a nod of the head and a click of the heels. Never bandy words with his ilk for he battens upon these and distorts them with relish to suit the digestion of his loquacity.

Then there are certain uncommunicative gentlemen who cannot be bothered using their brains and time to ponder questions. These are best left alone because under pressure they could wither you with words.

I recall the plight of a certain gentleman who once lost his way in a maze of country roads. He came upon a small man who was seated upon a milestone at the side of the road.

'Do you know such a place?' asked the man who had lost his way, naming a townland in the area.

'No,' said the man on the milestone. The lost man tendered other places and names but everytime he received a blunt negative. Finally the lost man lost his temper.

'What a fool,' he exploded, 'what an ass, what a lout.'

'Fool, yes,' said the man on the milestone, 'ass yes and lout yes but lost no.'

LADDER-HOLDING

Now I would like to explore new ground and for this reason I propose to deal with a subject which to my knowledge has never been dealt with before and that is, if you have not already guessed, the little known art of ladder-holding.

At the outset because it is relevant let me say that there is no such thing as a simple job of work. It may seem simple on the surface or it can be simply done when placed in the hands of competent people. The bother is that we tend to place our simple jobs in the hands of simple people and this is where the confusion arises. Because a job is simple and seemingly without complications we foolishly presume that anybody at all can be entrusted with it.

By anybody at all I mean those people who have been otherwise tried and found wanting, who have not been able to cope with jobs which called for skill and expertise, who, in short, can take a simple situation and confuse it irrevocably. There is no absence of physical or mental ability. It is just that the type of jobs to suit these particular types of people have not been devised yet.

Let us for the sake of argument create a situation where the point I am endeavouring to make can be clearly illustrated. Let us imagine, for instance, that our chimney needs to be cleaned and that it needs to be cleaned at once. Professional chimney sweeps are mainly itinerant or resident in cities where they are assured of full-time employment. Let us imagine, therefore, that the chimney which needs to be cleaned is not in a city and that there is no itinerant sweep available at the time. Logic and higher mathematics are called for here so we will proceed warily. Let us now make our first and most important deduction. In the absence of a qualified sweep we must, if there is to be a fire in the grate, entrust the job of sweeping to a part-time sweep or, in the event of no such person being available, to a competent person who has never swept a chimney before but is not afraid to have a go.

Before I proceed further let me say that the job does not have to be chimney cleaning. It might just as easily be a commission for the evisceration of eaves' shoots or the mere nailing down of a loose slate. What matters is that the use of a ladder is entailed, thus guaranteeing the emergence into our argument of a ladder-holder without whose presence we might as well abandon this entire treatise here and now. Our essay would be meaningless without him so let us look at him and his art from widely divergent angles and endeavour to arrive at a fair and worthy conclusion.

Your normal ladder-holder is an amiable, easy going fellow of mature years. He is totally devoid of temperament. In his job one dare not indulge in the irrational. There is too much at stake. The reason he is employed in the first place is because the person at the other end of the ladder is not fully conversant with its behaviour and needs all the moral support he can muster. Neither is he conversant with heights. Remember he is not a professional, that he is filling a gap. On the other hand the man at the bottom of the ladder is sure of his whereabouts. He has to be. He dare not commit himself to any sudden movement or move from his post for the barest fraction of a second. Should he do so the man at the top would suddenly be bereft of confidence and become prey to the thousand mishaps which lurk at the bases of unattended ladders. Fine if the man at the top is full of self-confidence. He will survive. If he is the opposite he is doomed.

That is why the role of ladder-holder is so important. He must at all times keep his head and be seen to be keeping his head. The best method of keeping a ladder steady is to place a leg on the first or second rung and both hands on the sides. This ensures a steady ladder at all times. Another important aspect is that an outward show of equanimity be available at all times to the man at the top whenever he looks down for re-assurance.

There is alas a type of ladder-holder who is given to gross exaggeration and histrionics when there is no justification whatsoever for same. Sometimes he manages to produce perspiration on his brow and consternation on his face as he holds on to the ladder for dear life at times shouting 'Oh, oh' and 'Oops' as if the man at the top were in danger of his life and that, but for him, the ladder-holder, catastrophe would be inevitable.

Fortunately, show-offs like these do not last long in a business which calls for unrelenting application. They are soon spotted and struck off.

For a long time now there has been much debate as to who suffers the greater risk, the man at the top or the man at the bottom of the ladder. On the surface it would seem that the man at the top is subject to all the risk and the man at the bottom to none. Let us suppose that the man at the top falls off and ask ourselves where he is most likely to fall. The answer is that he is most likely to fall on top of the man at the bottom, thus breaking his own fall at the expense of the ladder-holder. All that can happen to the man at the top is that he may fall down whereas the ladder-holder is threatened from several areas. There is the danger of falling slates, eave's shoots loam, dislodged plaster and broken chimney pots to mention but a few. There is too the not-infrequent incidence of the man at the top slipping as he climbs down. It is a known fact that ladder-users are not nearly as careful climbing down a ladder as they are climbing up. If they slip they cannot but fall on the man at the bottom. So now we may reverse a long-held tenet which would have us believe that the man at the top of the ladder is a more important part of the unit than the man at the bottom. From the evidence I have submitted even the most bigoted reader will be forced to agree that the man holding the ladder is the more important.

The moral here, of course, is that things are never what they seem. Please bear this in mind the next time you pass under a ladder and spare a thought for those who for too long have endured the thin end of the wedge.

*   *   *   *   *

HUMMING

Before commencing this essay I went through considerable soul-searching. My initial idea was to dash off seven or eight hundred words on the subject of humming. Alas I made the fatal mistake of confiding to a friend.

'What about hawing?' he said at once. The remark set me off course. The writing of an essay is a delicate business. One has to unequivocal and precise. Ambiguity and ambivalence are out. Thus we must agree that a distinction has to be drawn and the question that must be asked is this:

'Can there be humming without hawing?'

Those who combine humming and hawing will hold one view while those who hum without hawing will hold another. My view is that humming is a legitimate and independent transmission of carefully considered inner thought whereas hawing is but a mere part or fraction of a greater whole. For instance one can haw-haw, he-haw and hum-haw but a haw without a hum, a hee or another haw is meaningless and cannot be said to compound a meaningful utterance. Having made this clear we are now free to concern ourselves solely with humming.

Your committed hummer is, of course, a spoiled singer. By committed hummer I mean he who hums whole songs rather than snatches. Your casual hummer is just another man who wants to say no and is merely softening the blow. Then there is the one-note hummer.

He is a man who is asked a simple question but by virtue of a quirky make-up is unable to give a simple answer. He hums away in subdued monotone hoping that the person who has asked the question will grow tired and go away.

Failing this he silently prays that the listener will deduce some sort of satisfactory answer from the sum of his hums and settle for this in the absence of anything more tangible.

The type of hummer who irritates me most would be best delineated by the following example. Many years ago my mother commissioned a handy man to clean our eaves' shoots. He arrived with a bucket, a ladder and an assistant. Before they started she asked them if they would like a cup of tea. The pair emitted a series of abbreviated but conformable hums and when questioned a second time treated us with longer and seemingly more thoughtful hums. We deduced that they would indeed like a cup of tea. In answer to subsequent requests such as whether they would like bread and butter, jam, cold meat etc., they conspired to lead us on with the same disarming hums.

They spent most of the day doing the job and when they finished late in the afternoon I was entrusted with the task of finding out how much was due them. I was answered with hums long and short and much serious shaking of heads. This latter was to imply that the amount might be more than was usual, when I repeated the question I failed to elicit an answer. All I got was another dose of hums. The going rate per day at the time was ten bob so I asked them if this would be alright. This drew forth a babble of hums, unprecedented in range and depth. In the end we were forced to pay them twelve and six-pence per skull and although they said neither yes nor no to any of our offers.

Do not for a moment be so foolish as to believe that this sort of humming is a refuge for the inarticulate. Far from it. Hummers of the type I have mentioned have learned over the years that a meaningless answer can be extremely intimidating. They give the impression that they are being badgered when a simple question is being repeated for the second or third time. The only way to deal with these evasive and demanding types is to hum back at them. It never fails.

Now let us turn our attention to the musical hummer. I had my first taste of musical humming at a 'Feis Cheoil' when I was ten. There was in our class choir a sweet-faced boy who had an equally sweet soprano voice. At the 'Feis Cheoil' he would sing *Danny Boy* and we would back him up with gentle humming.

He got all the credit. We got none. All this went to his head and at one 'Feis' instead of commencing with *O Danny Boy* he started with *O Daniel Boy*. This unexpected grandeur threw us completely and the ensuing humming was a shambles. The boy soprano's voice broke at the same time and so ended my career as a competitive hummer.

If the gentle reader is truly interested in seeking the source of really genuine humming, i. e. humming which is musically expressive and yet linguistically effective, he should ask one of his relatives or friends for the loan of a substantial sum of money.

The answer to such a request is the source of all that is practical and realistic in expressive humming.

*   *   *   *   *

THE DRINKING FIELDS

Men who grow anxious for intoxicating drink for reasons which cannot easily be analysed are very often the victims of intolerance and misunderstanding. When I was younger people were more tolerant and when neighbours overdrank you would hear remarks like the following:

'Wisha the poor man is plagued by drought', or 'God help him he's cursed with a terrible tooth for porter.' Those charitable souls of yesteryear never inflicted the hard word when a soft one was admissable.

It must be conceded, however, in these days of affluence, wantonness, permissiveness, etc., that drinking is a more serious problem that ever before and that we should look above and beyond the accepted norms for the root causes of this much-abused practice.

Recent disclosures in the National Press about the drinking habits of the Irish people will not have escaped the notice of my readers. That they are true is near enough to fact but a very heavy reduction on the per capita consumption must be allowed on the grounds that we have a large tourist intake not to mention all those buck navvies (of whom I was once a proud member) who come home annually and bi-annually and whose recreation time is spent, in the main, in public houses. For reasons unknown these navvies and their adherents have never been regarded as tourists. A probable reason could well be that they spend too much to be looked upon as such. I have known many who spent several hundred pounds in the few weeks available to them, not always on themselves alone but on the many short-term admirers that a flahool hand can attract.

I will not go into the reasons given for the Irish obsession with intoxicating liquor in the most recent published analyses. I have my own theory about these and I have drawn the conclusion, from long practical experience, that our heavy drinking has to do with landscape. Do I hear sniggers?

Let there be sniggers but it should be remembered that I have as much right to put forward my theories about the causes behind the national pastime as anybody. Recently I took a break from the booze. I decided to forego my nightly indulgence to honour the memory of a departed parent. I endured the martyrdom for a month which, when you make allowance for the resistance of the subject, is a reasonable period of abstention. I might not have gone back on the stuff for a much longer period if it had not been for a certain incident which dampened my fortitude.

I am in the habit most evenings of taking a walk through a number of boggy fields outside the town. I intrude upon nobody save the occasional snipe who must only benefit from these incursions of mine if he is to be fully alert for the day when fowlers will threaten his very existence.

On this particular afternoon I stopped for a moment or two to savour a few lungfuls of country air. Between breaths I thought I heard a whisper, a sort of subdued, caressing sibilance from somewhere behind me. I looked around but could see nothing. The whispering persisted and shortly I learned that it was coming from everywhere. It was the earth itself and it wasn't whispering. It was drinking. Earlier it the day there had been a number of heavy showers and the noise which sounded so like whispering was the squelchy earth swallowing copious draughts of refreshing rainwater. In short the soggy fields were soaking it up goodo. It was an unmistakeable sound and it brought back happy memories of intoxicating beverages which I had so often quaffed myself.

To make a long story short there arose inside me an irrepressible longing for a long and a strong drink of bodied beer in rich quantity to freshen my exhausted fibres and restore to them their old pulpy satiety.

I place the blame fair and squarely on the drinking fields and had it not been for the convivial whispers under the grasses I might have passed on and inflicted further needless tyranny upon my rapidly dehydrating body.

These particular fields are always drinking. Morning, noon and night they absorb moisture. Even in the height of summer they absorb the dews of night and morning and dry as the weather may be they lap up left-over dampness deep down where the sun can't get at it.

To hear them at their best you would want to pay them a visit after three or four days of heavy rain. Then the noise is almost deafening provided you are prepared to give it your undivided attention. I always say *Slainte* when I hear these fields indulging thus.

This then could well be one of the undisclosed causes which might explain our predilection for alcoholic beverages to the degree which makes us stand out above other nations. Shakespeare had the same thing to say about Denmark. Correct me if I'm wrong:

This heavy-headed revel East and West
Which makes us traduced and taxed of other nations.

I hope that what I have unfolded will be taken seriously. To those who are forever seeking messages I would say that it would be wiser for an alcoholically-inclined person to steer clear of drinking fields and confine himself to the public highway.

*   *   *   *   *

IT NEVER RAINS BUT IT POURS

Ever since I was a boy I have been fascinated by the pronouncements and conclusions of local weather-forecasters. These men knew their suns and moons, their winds and skies but were modest in the extreme about their accomplishments.

'Tis many a long day now since myself and Mickeen McCarthy borrowed Jack Horan's ass to draw a four-man slean of turf out of Dirha Bog. On our way we met Sir Stafford Cripps and Mr Chamberlain which were the names given to two elderly brothers who dwelt in the farthest-in house in the bog.

'Will the day hold fine?' Mickeen asked. Sir Stafford raised wrinkled eyes to the western horizon and sniffed the wind.

'There's no rain in that,' he said and he turned to the brother for corroboration.

'The crows are flying with their backs to the wind.' Mr Chamberlain announced, 'and by all the powers that be you'll get no rain today.' The next soul we encountered was Sonny Canavan and he making horse stoolins of dry turf on a bank near the roadway.

'Will the day hold fine?' Mickeen asked.

'Would I be here?' Canavan asked, 'but for I knowing we'll have no break.' This gave us great heart because the Ballybunion Pattern Day which is the fifteenth of August was only two days off and Mickeen had a buyer lined up for the turf if we could have it on the side of the road by evening.

'Listen,' said Canavan and he raised a finger for silence.

We listened and far away from the west came a sullen deep monotone interspersed with the faint cries of far-off sea mews.

'What does it signify?' Mickeen McCarthy asked.

'It signifies,' said Canavan, 'that the sea is near today and when the sea is near you'll see no break.'

Greatly heartened Mickeen produced a paper packet of Woodbines and tendered one each to Canavan and myself. We then sat on our behinds, our backs supported by the stoolins and our legs stretched in front of us, content in the knowledge that we had the day long to handle the job before us. We spoke about the war. The following day Churchill and Roosevelt were to meet at sea. Earlier that year Hess had flown to Scotland.

'If Hess had landed in Dirha instead of Scotland,' said Canavan, 'we'd have an extra man for the slean and we needn't be recruiting townies.'

Earlier that year, as well, the *Bismark* had been sunk.

'I'll tell ye once and I'll tell ye no more,' said Canavan, 'that Hitler lost his chance. He got his fine days too but he didn't make hay.'

So the conversation went on and on until the shrouded sun begain to rise in the noonday sky. We took our leave of Canavan who returned to his stoolins and we made haste for the house of Jack Horan. At either side of the roadway the larks rose singing and the mellow booming of bullfrogs bore witness to the simple jobs of bogland life. Now and then a billy goat would raise his head from the herbiage to inspect us and mild, summer breezes rustled the tinder-dry heather.

'These are mighty times,' said Mickeen. At Jack Horan's we were greeted by his wife who told us that himself was in bed but that we could have the loan of the ass for five woodbines. The cigarettes were handed over and we set about tackling up.

'Will it hold fine?' Mickeen asked of Mrs Horan.

'Will it hold fine Jack?' she called through the bedroom window. There was no immediate answer but after a short while Jack Horan emerged in a long nightshirt down to his toes and a cap on his head. There was a cigarette in his mouth. The ass was now tackled and the rail in place.

'Will it hold fine?' Mickeen asked. Jack Horan took the cigarette from his mouth, topped it and carefully placed the butt behind his left ear.

'Look beyond,' he said and he pointed a black-nailed finger towards where the blue mountains of the Dingle range stood out from the background of a clear sky.

'When the wind is from that quarter,' said Jack Horan, 'the weather will stay settled.' Along the bumpy roadway we walked at either side of the plodding ass. The larks sang louder now and soared exultantly heavenwards leaving behind them wonderful trails of song. Suddenly I was struck on the forehead by a solitary, outsized raindrop. A minute passed and I was struck by another. Then came another and another until it seemed that every raindrop in the sky had specially convened for an all-out assault on Dirha Bog. The rain came down in blinding sheets now until streams began to flow at either side of the roadway. The ass slithered and fell and the passage which led to our slean of turf had now become a gurgling stream.

'Never mind,' said Mickeen, 'we still have a smoke left.'

From his pocket he produced a paper packet of woodbines but, inside, the cigarettes were wet and soggy as bog-mould.

'It was said before,' Mickeen announced, 'but I'll say it again. It never rains but it pours.'

*　　*　　*　　*　　*

FARMERS' SONS

Earlier in this book we dealt with farmers' boys and I think we covered most of the ground which is common to this subject. Let us now press on and deal with cases of similar hardship amongst farmers' sons and other associate members of the rural scene when money was not as plentiful as it is now and slave labour was as common in the countryside as dossing is presently. Let me say here and now that I do not look upon those who peruse these pages of mine as mere readers. Far from it. I look upon them, whether they be old or young, as students of the passing scene and not just the passing scene alone but as undergraduates in the university of things unusual and as scholars devoted to the preservation of past cultures and refinements. Having said this we may feel free to press on.

There were in the twenties and thirties and the earlier forties in this green and pleasant land a substantial number of equally substantial farmers who expected all those of their own households to work around the clock where possible and, where not, as hard as possible for as long as possible. Fair play to them they worked hard themselves but that was more or less to be expected since the land they worked was their own. It was different with their wives, daughters, sons and any others who might happen to be dependant for the bite and sup on these agrestic Simon Legrees.

While such domineering taskmasters were inclined to tolerate crimes like murder, rape and incest with good-natured tolerance they could not and would not tolerate the sin of idleness. Consequently, if they saw a member of

51

the household in a motionless or unoccupied state they immediately sought to see him working at some task no matter how meaningless that task might seem. To them idleness was a sin and should be flayed ruthlessly at every hand's turn. For instance there was nothing to stop a man with two broken legs from stitching an ass's harness nor a woman heavy with child from cutting seed potatoes.

I personally knew of a farmer who was so opposed to idleness that he did not confine his war against it to the household alone. Even idle animals got under his skin and there is the case of the Rhode Island Red cock who was knocked down by a drunken cyclist. The creature had its legs broken and as a result was unable to accommodate the many hens and chickens who expected to be facilitated whenever the notion caught them. The wife of the farmer in question tied splints to the broken legs and allowed the cock to convalesce. The following day the farmer saw him squatting impotently in the fowl-run. He caught the luckless invalid by both wings and transferred him to the fowl-house where he sat him on top of a clutch of eggs. There he remained until the eggs were fully hatched and the use of his legs returned to him. Needless to say that same cock kept an ever-alert eye for drunken cyclists after that. There is nothing so humiliating for a Rhode Island Red cock as to have to sit on a clutch of eggs. In human terms it is much the same as putting a full-blooded Lothario in charge of a nursery.

Snoring also was regarded as an evil of great magnitude. Snoring suggests restfulness and contentment and where you have restfulness and contentment you have no progress. Nothing gets done until the snoring dies away and the snorer resurrects himself from his place of repose. Let me say here that night-time snoring was considered to be legitimate by most rural employers of the time. It was day-snoring that unsettled them and they were ever on the alert for it. Farmers' boys and farmers' sons were not above stealing a few winks of sleep following a late night. Consequently they would throw themselves down with abandon in haysheds, in the lee of hedges, in meadows and other shady places for the purpose of seizing upon forty or so winks in order to refurbish tattered nerves and rejuvenate weary limbs. At the first sign of a snore the farmer would raise his head like a bull searching for interlopers among his cows and heifers. After that he would devote his undivided attention to the likely source of the snore. Having been young himself he would, of course, be well acquainted with the most likely snore resorts. Upon discovering the area he would roar at the top of his voice at the unfortunate snorer, drag him to his feet and implant a mighty kick on that part of the anatomy known as the posterior.

These men, therefore, were as we have tried to show, totally opposed to five day weeks, half-days and holy days, bank holidays, pattern days and any and all other days devoted to rest, religion and recreation as opposed to normal working days. Most of them died prematurely from hurry and worry while those who were opposed to their strictures lived long and happy lives even in this world.

*   *   *   *   *

'PLENTY COTTON'

Recently I was asked by one of my sons if I could tell him what was meant by the expression 'Plenty Cotton'. I was happy indeed to be able to answer in the affirmative because I recalled that the expression was in wide use around that time when you could buy a narrow bottle of superfine brilliantine hair-oil for tuppence and when a great majority of country people were still suspicious of tomatoes.

The expression 'Plenty Cotton' was first used by the late Dan Paddy Andy O'Sullivan the famous Lyreacrompane matchmaker to a group of Irish army privates and noncoms who stood shyly outside the entrance to his famous dance-hall one warm Sunday night in 1941.

In those days several hundred troops were camped in Lyreacrompane. They spent their days cutting and saving turf in the surrounding bogs and their nights in search of women and other simple diversions. The pay was in the region of a pound a week so it will be seen that it was absolutely necessary to manufacture home-made entertainment if they were to remain mentally stable.

These 'Emergency Men' were nearly all volunteers who supplemented the meagre battalions of regulars when it was felt that Ireland was in danger of invasion. They were young men in their teens drawn in the main from the adjacent counties of Cork and Limerick. They were the cream of the country but they were as green as their uniforms and many of them had never seen the inside of a dancehall before.

As I have already intimated they stood in a circle around the front and only door of the dancehall, their uniforms spick and span, listening with a newly-born yearning to the romantic strains of *South of the Border* which was the rage at the time or to *Let Him Go Let Him Tarry* if the three-man orchestra happened to be subscribing to that novelty of novelties, the foxtrot.

Dan Paddy Andy, if business was slack, would come to the door of the hall and call out to the eager-faced troops: 'Come on in lads, plenty cotton here.'

This was to suggest that there were women in plenty inside since simple cotton dresses were the dance frocks that prevailed at the time.

In those days dress dances were confined to places such as Duhallow and like spots and went under the misleading nomenclature of Hunt Balls. Be that as it may it is with the expression 'Plenty Cotton' that we are now dealing. What nicer method of describing an abundance of the opposite sex. As I recall there were less poetic descriptions at that time. They were known as pieces of skirt, totties, dolls, birds and long-hairs to mention but a few. Dan Paddy Andy, at least, had pride in the feminine produce of the local countryside and was determined that they should not be degraded by ill-becoming names.

This is not to suggest that they wore cotton dresses alone. Far from it. A few of the older girls wore corsets but these were in a minority. The standard apparel was your cotton frock underneath which was a slip, a chemise, a chastity cord and a doughty pair of long, sensible bloomers designed to withstand any onslaught which, God forbid, might take place in the heat of the moment when a couple might find themselves alone with no company save the sedge and rush and no sound save the base booming of the mating bullfrog. Apart from the bleating of the jacksnipe and the distant barking of dogs these were the only sounds to be heard in the happy countryside.

Inside the hall was a large paraffin lamp which was ideal for such a situation as its light was weak and consequently more inducive to romance. In fact there was a song of the period which contained the line: 'Don't you know it's more romantic when the lights are low.'

The prevailing odour, if one were to discount the sweet and transient whiffs of 'Outdoor Girl' or 'Pond's Powder', was that of paraffin oil.

Paraffin mixed with dance crystals or grated wax candles was also used to make the floor 'skeety'. In those days boys and girls would dance till they were drenched with sweat and happily exhausted from a score or more of consecutive dances.

From time to time I meet middle-aged men who were soldiers in Lyreacrompane in the early forties. They all speak nostalgically of those halcyon days and nights and they will remind you emphatically that there was no place like Dan Paddy Andy's dancehall and no sport like the sport they had then.

There is one man in particular who ended up a sergeant in that army who lives presently in the city. The last time I met him he told me that he has a recurring dream. There he is, a raw recruit, a mere gorsoon, with his cap perched jauntily on the side of his head and he standing with a crowd of his fellows listening to the music which floated outwards and upwards to enchant him. Always from the past comes the voice of Dan Paddy Andy: 'Come on in lads, plenty cotton here.'

*   *   *   *   *

BOG-LATIN

Long ago in north Kerry there was a man by the name of Paddy Brolly. He worked for two elderly brothers on a middling-sized farm which was situated a mile and a half at the other side of the Back-of-Beyond. He lived in the farmhouse with the brothers and all got on well together. The motor car and the telephone and the electric light were the chief reasons for the decline and fall of that happy and peaceful clime known as the Back-of-Beyond and sad to say this is the first time its passing has ever been recorded in print.

Let us press on, however, and find out why this man Paddy Brolly should be mentioned in our tale. Let me say that it was my intention at the outset to devote this treatise to Bog-Latin, a now-extinct language which flourished for a while in Irish country places in spite of persecution by church, state and several drunken school-masters who should have known better. On second thoughts, however, I realised that no discourse on Bog-Latin would be complete without mention of Brolly. He was a simple man with minor aspirations. A sufficiency of porter, meat and tobacco with the odd hoult of a willing woman were his total ambitions. Yet it is widely believed that it was his demise which gave rise to the birth of Bog-Latin.

When Paddy Brolly died the brothers who employed him sent for the priest. Instead of going themselves they commissioned a fool to tell the priest that he was wanted to bury Paddy Brolly. When the fool arrived at the presbytery he told the priest that Paddy Brolly wanted to see him.

'For what?' the priest asked.

'He wants to see you because he's dead,' said the fool,

57

'and that's why.' No wonder then that the priest cleared the fool from his doorstep. When the fool arrived back he told the brothers that the priest refused to come.

'We'll bury him ourselves.' said the older of the brothers. 'All we're short of is Latin. We have the Holy Water and we can lay him out in his Clydesdale,'(i. e. name given to navy blue Sunday suits of the period).

On the day of the funeral there was a good attendance. When the coffin was lowered into the grave a neighbour came forward and shook the Holy Water on top of it. For good measure she gave everyone within range a sprinkling also. The older of the two brothers stepped forward and said a few simple prayers. Then he spoke through his nose in what he believed to be good quality Latin. All the Latin he knew was what he picked up in dribs and drabs from Masses high and low and funerals down the years.

'*Dominum novarum in saecula saeculorum,*' he opened. Members of the gathering looked at him with new-found respect. Encouraged he went on, '*Dominus vobiscum in nomine patternum tatarara eternibus sanctibus terra firma. Adoremus temus cum spiritu sanctus amen.*'

'*Latine dictum,*' said a scholar who happened to be in attendance. '*Et cum spirtu tuo,*' the older brother gave answer and with that the mourners went to the nearest pub to drown their sorrows.

After that Bog-Latin was in wide use and there was great 'sanctimussing' and 'saccalarum-saccaloring' whenever the opportunity presented itself. It was the clergy, incidentally, who christened it Bog-Latin. Those who used it simply called it 'oremussing'. The *sean-daoine* used to say that it broke out in people who should have been priests but were not for one reason or another. Bog-Latin spread as far as America but only a man with a west of Ireland accent was capable of uttering its nuances in the true traditional manner.

Bog-Latin gave birth to quite a few phrases. There was for instance 'Bladderum Barum' and 'coaxiorum'. The latter was widely used as a love potion. 'Bladderum Barum' was a send-the-fool-farther composition in the same league as the glass hammer and the round square.

Time past and many blessings sprung from this unique language. There was the blessing bestowed upon young men and women emigrating to America, England and elsewhere which went as follows: *'Julia, Johanna, Manacka, Cassumboola junka'* and there was the blessing bestowed upon people who were afraid to go home late at night after wren-dances, hoolies and card gambles. Both hands were placed upon the head of the recipient and the following was intoned sanctimoniously: *'In caporetis is taus is coc maggeg is omnibus nostrum saculata.'*

Over the years the great sayings became diluted and corrupted because no one went to the bother of compiling a Bog-Latin dictionary. The final blow came when a yank by the name of Paddy Fongtu came on holiday to the west. His father had been a Paddy Enright from Tubberclarig but his mother was a Lily Fongtu from Kwei Yang, China. He stayed with relations and one night at a wren-dance he overheard a Bog-Latin blessing. Full of drink he insisted in giving a blessing of his own which went like this:

Me ackey bo-bo. Velly good so-so.
Me lika Lilya. She lika me.
Me filiongkong. Fatty man come along
Steali allabooli from Poo Chinee.

A Bronx-born pensioner who happened to be in the vicinity informed those present that what Paddy Fongtu had chanted so ceremoniously was no more than a children's street-song in Chinatown, New York. Thus ended the great era of Bog-Latin, now alas heard no more and becoming less than a memory when once it held its own with the best. *Omnibus nostrum sacculata.*

HUMMING – PART TWO

In an earlier discourse which dealt with humming as distinct from humming and hawing we examined the musical aspects of humming as well as the linguistic. I confess that we did not delve very deeply on the occasion but this was a deliberate deflection on my part as I did not desire to immerse the beginner too deeply, as it were, in the bottomless waters of this disputatious subject.

We will now, therefore, turn aside from the elementary phases and in part two we will examine the art of humming from hitherto unauthenticated sources and unmeasured angles. I would advise the reader to take off his hat and overcoat at this stage as I want nothing to obscure the view.

Let us start out this evening with clerical humming which is about as advanced a form of humming as you would be like to find in a country such as ours which, as we are constantly reminded, is largely Catholic as distinct from largely Christian. Clerical humming is not confined to the pulpit and indeed it is my contention that it flourishes best in the confines of the confessional. Not all confessors are hummers. Some are hawers, ha-haers and ho-hoers while others still are finger fidgeters, nose-pullers and lip pursers. We must not concern ourselves with these. Let us look instead to the humming priest, not to be confused with the singing priest who is of recent vintage and very often cannot function without a guitar.

My first encounter with a clerical hummer came when I was eighteen. The Redemptorists were giving a week-long retreat in the town and on the penultimate night I went to confession. I had been away for a considerable time and so

I entered the box with some trepidation.

The priest listened patiently while I reeled off my sins. When I was half-way through he opened with a series of short hums. Then he paused. At first I was terrifed lest he refuse me absolution.

When I hesitated he started to hum secondly. These were egging, encouraging, entreating hums. He could not have been more articulate. I deduced that he was telling me not to worry, that it was not the end of the world, that all would be well and that absolution was at hand. I was correct. Afterwards I met another clerical hummer although truth to tell he was as much a bawler as he was a hummer. When I confessed my first sin he hummed briefly and pleasantly. When I confessed my second he hummed loudly and less pleasantly. When I confessed my third I was absolutely convinced that he had turned into an enraged bull so fiercely did he bawl. Presently, however, he calmed down and hummed away with variations as I recited the closing lines of my more recent transgressions.

Some deaf priests were greatly addicted to humming in moderation as the penitents recited their offences. This was to give the impression that they weren't deaf at all but were indicating by the volume, timbre and nuances of their humming what they thought of each particular sin. As often as not they hummed severely for a mere venial and quite tolerantly for a grevious mortal. In those days deaf priests were extremely popular and people would travel long distances to be shriven by them.

Let us now by way of contrast have a look at musical humming. Let us take an example. There was a middle-aged man who used to live in our street who was most anxious to get married but was not possessed of the requisite acumen to first isolate and then propose to a suitable girl. He was the despair of the street for years. Finally somebody decided that a match should be made for him. An obliging neighbour was commissioned to do the job. He called at the bachelor's house and after the usual preamble asked him if he would be interested in settling down with a certain girl. The answer was a colourless, discouraging meaningless hum. He gave the same response as other females were suggested. Name after name was reeled off and then quite unexpectedly at the mention of a girl called Nora Spillane the bachelor gave vent to a sonorous, high-pitched, enduring bout of humming. He had made his choice. The couple were married and there wasn't a hum nor a haw out of the pair of them for the rest of their lives.

Before the advent of moving pictures, television and bingo, hummers were in wide demand in the countryside. Although not nearly as important as crownawners, keeners or diddlers they were nevertheless most welcome at events such as wren-dances and American wakes. They were, however, substitutes rather than star performers but their roles must not be underestimated on this account.

A good hummer generally made a good husband. Instead of answering back he would hum out his feelings unintelligibly thereby giving no offence and if a child was fretful or wakeful it was no bother to him to hum the infant into a sound sleep.

If he was romantically inclined he could hum snatches from acceptable love-songs thereby inducing an amorous condition in the heart of his beloved and greatly reducing the odds against rejection.

In the face of misfortune he could keep his mouth shut and hum away as if all was well. Thereby he could instil confusion in the minds of his detractors and give a feeling of security to those who were his own. Finally let me echo the sentiments of the late Hummer Moran who was so-called because he died humming.

'Better,' said he, 'to have hummed and made a heims of it than never to have hummed at all.'

CREAKY STEPS

There used to be a creaky step on the stairs of the house where I was born and reared. As an alarm system it was without equal and no matter how carefully one trod on it, it always reacted noisily.

It was a step for which I had no love but nothing would induce my father or mother to have it repaired.

'That step, ' said my father, 'always informs me of the homecoming hours of my sons.'

It was indeed a third party. It was also a traitorous double-crossing slat of timber which creaked ominously and often cockily when one of us was out longer than he should.

We used to try avoiding it but somehow it succeeded in passing on the information to the next step which creaked informatively, no matter how light one's footfall. This led me to believe, and I have no reason since to doubt it, that all stairs, great and small are possessed of this single traitorous step.

My father was proud of our step. In his eyes the other steps in the flight were common fellows not worthy of notice. Years afterwards when we had grown up 'and gone our separate ways in the world he still cherished the step and refused to replace it and events proved he was right for the step was to fulfil a role similar to that played by the Capitol geese when they saved Rome or Killorglin's puck goat when he forewarned his friends and neighbours of approaching invaders.

It was the second night of Listowel Races and my mother and he were fast asleep. Night is not quite correct since it was two o'clock in the morning but you know how people say night when they really mean morning. For instance the song: 'Who were you with last night?' should I have no doubt, read: 'Who were you with this morning?' If the girl in question was home before twelve, the song would not have been written. Nobody minds a girl having a night out but a morning out is a different matter.

But where was I?

Yes, it was two o'clock in the morning and my father was snoring away to his heart's content. He was, as snorers go, in a class of his own. In this respect the Tonic Solfa held no terrors for him and he cavorted between high do and low do like an apprentice operatic singer.

Sound asleep as he was, when the step creaked he awoke immediately and seized a poker which he always kept handy. He did not go out on the stairs but called out from the safety of the room.

'Who's there?' he shouted.

No answer at first but when the step creaked again he knew that the invader was at least intimidated and contemplating retreat. My father waited a few moments and then went out on the landing, clutching the poker. He was, it is only fair to say, followed by my mother.

'There's nobody there!' she said.

'Correction!' said my father; 'you mean there's nobody there now!'

'Maybe 'twas the cat?' my mother suggested.

'Nonsense!' said my father. 'No cat could cause a creak like that.'

Months later, when we were all at home for Christmas he told us about the incident. He gave a description of the intruder. 'The scoundrel must have weighed fifteen or sixteen stone,' he said. 'He was also remarkably fit, either a wrestler or a fighter.' My father deduced all this from the two creaks. 'But for that step,' he concluded, 'we would all have been murdered in our beds.'

'There was only the two of us in the house!' said my

mother.

'When I said "all of us" I meant the two of us,' my father announced.

The following night, St Stephen's Night, the step betrayed us individually and collectively as we entered at all hours from dances and parties. My father didn't really mind the time but he liked to know what was going on.

I have on my own stairs a similar step and sometimes, when I go to football matches, the missus says: 'If I'm asleep when you come back, don't wake me up!' I promise I will do this and always I keep my promise. But one night the step creaked and she woke up. I spent the next two hours describing the match. In the end she asked; 'What woke me?' I told her it was a creaky step. 'Nonsense,' she said. 'We have no creaky step.' I left the room and told her to listen. When I came up to the step in question it creaked in a most objectionable manner. When I returned to the room, she was satisfied.

'You know. . . ,' she said, before she went to sleep.

'What's that?' I asked.

'Nothing,' she said, 'but it's just that I've always wanted a creaking step in the house.'

I like the step myself because it is more than likely that it will be an asset to me, the same as my father's was to him. A creaking step is as good as a dog and it eats very little — just a fragment of wax-polish now and then.

*   *   *   *   *

DUMP GULLS

I am a man who loves the seashore. I love the lapping of small waves as much as I do the thunder of great ones. I love the ozone and I breathe it in the way a famished whale savours its first mighty swallow of plankton. I love the spirit of the sea and its undying restlessness. Byron speaks for me when he says in 'Childe Harold':

> Roll on thou deep and dark blue ocean roll.
> Ten thousand fleets sweep over thee in vain.
> Man marks the earth with ruin, his control
> Stops with the shore upon thy watery plain.

I love the awesome power of the storm and I feel in tune with the seabirds as they wheel and plunge and soar and drift and glide, loving the strong wind and using it to hover, dive or climb. Their cries above the roaring of wind and wave delight me for these are cries of an ecstasy that man cannot comprehend. In human speech they would be saying: 'Look at me. I am a bird of the air. I have mastered the wind. I spurn the earth. I know no confines. I am the loveliest of God's created creatures. Mine is the loveliest of all motions. I outdo ballet in my grace. I am majestic.'

So well might they boast for they who are speechless are compensated by the wonderful gift of flight. I wish I had the space to go on and on and to dwell upon cormorant, guillemot and oyster-catcher to mention but a few of those of our feathered friends who live by the seashore but I have a duty to my readers and so I will deal with what are loosely referred to as seagulls and about one of whom Gerald Griffin had the following to say:

White bird of the tempest, oh beautiful thing
With the bosom of snow and the motionless wing.

If Gerald Griffin were to come with me upon one of my daily walks he would not be long in revising his opinion of the seagull. Most of these 'beautiful things' have long ago abandoned the sea for town dumps and places where entrails, trash and other refuse is thrown. Here you will find them in unbelievable numbers, these once proud seafarers, squawking and infighting over scraps like hyenas. They have forsaken the glinting cliff faces for the smelly, sickly, ugly dumping grounds of town and city. They rise bleating and shrieking every so often for no reason that is apparent and sometimes they are not above assaulting an innocent pedestrian without provocation of any sort. In winter-time when frost is rife and food is scarce they are not above attacking children and making off with whatever it is that the child happens to be eating at the time. Seagulls my hat. Dump-gulls is a more appropriate name and they should be referred to by this name until such time as they return to their natural haunts and leave scavenging to the scavengers. I, therefore, propose that we call them henceforth by the name of dump-gull until such time as they abandon their evil ways and return to their once proud calling as princes of seaside places.

Worst of all I have heard and seen them arguing with common crows. The pandemonium over the snatching of infinitesimal food particles is deafening. No self-respecting seabird should be seen arguing with a crow. Crows are the clowns of the bird world, the rapscallions and the thieves and to be seen in argument with them is a sign of idiocy.

Let me at once absolve the many fine species of gull who have stayed in their native places, who have not been and will not be lured by the easy pickings of town dumps and backyards, proud sea-mews who have ridden out tempest after tempest and who would mew with disdain at the thought of foresaking their natural habitats for the refuse ground of wingless humans.

It is the dump-gull's squawking to which I most object. It has, in its new confines, reached hysterical proportions and the sad musical beauty of their seashore crying is now no more. Oh what a falling-off there is. There is a lesson for the human here. Do not be in too much of a hurry to foresake your native place for the allure of distant cities or faraway lands. It is better to be king of the mountain and marsh than another digit in another ghetto. Just as the once-noble seabird said goodbye to his natural terrain so too did many fine and noble humans. They swapped the beauty, the simplicity and the frugality of moor and mountain for crowded places to squabble for more and still more until they have become sated with false values and no longer know how to live meaningful lives.

But enough. It is with the seagull that we must concern ourselves and not to forget that he is no longer entitled to that name. He is a dump-gull and will remain a dump-gull until he turns his face to the sea once more.

*   *   *   *   *

BADGES

Why is it that men who wear badges are nearly always the proprietors of sterner and soberer miens than those who wear no badges at all? If you don't believe me look about you. A man of one or more badges will be seen to be less flippant, less fugacious and less feckless than his badgeless contemporaries. Could it be that he is conscious of an added responsibility, that he is aware of a new dimension, that he is the physical embodiment of what the badge stands for or is it because I who am without a badge am self-conscious and, as a result, deferential?

A man wears a badge because he wishes to announce publicly his affiliation to or sympathy with certain organisations and points of view and just as surely as you'll see a badge in favour of one thing you'll see a badge in favour of the opposite except, of course, in the case of those who entertain moderate opinions. Badges, in a sense, are like colours at football matches. There isn't much point in having black if there is no white, in having green if there is no red and so forth and so on. Those who sport colours are expressing pride in their counties or countries and are generally harmless sorts while those who wear no identifying colour are often far more partisan. The same cannot always be said of badges but it is fair to assume that a man who publicly wears a badge has not all that much to hide even if he pretends otherwise.

Do not for a moment get the impression that I am opposed to badges. Far from it. The more the merrier. What worries me is the prospect of too many badges. I tremble at the thought of a personality completely subject to the demands of a badge.

Men wear flowers, shamrocks and palms so why no badges? If all men were equal there would be no need for badges.

A man is easily identified by the badge he wears and while it is not as accurate as an identity tag it tells us a good deal about him, not everything but enough to help us in establishing an attitude towards him. There are some who wear badges at the backs of their lapels rather than the front where everybody can see them. There are a number of reasons why men do this. One of the commoner is that they are at liberty to flash the badge to others who wear it publicly and obviously are in full sympathy with whatever cause it stands for. To those who are opposed to the sentiments expressed by the badge no offence is given because it is not visible. These *Tadhg a'da thaobh* types have a powerful instinct for survival but often, because they endeavour to keep in with everybody, they have the support of nobody.

Then there are temporary and permanent badges. For example under the head of permanent might come pioneer pins, Fainni nua and sean-fhainni, anti-swear pins, blood donor pins etcetera, while under the head of temporary might come Shamrock sprigs, palms, team emblems, carnations, Easter Lilies etcetera. Believe it or not I have seen as many as five of these occupying the same lapel. I have seen a Fainne Nua, an Easter Lily, a blood donor pin and two shrivelled, decaying remnants of blessed palm and Shamrock left over from preceeding Holy Days.

A fine thing this, a rare form of loyalty which suggests too a sporting type of fellow who is prepared to stand back from nothing.

We can learn much from men who wear badges which are out of vogue. Let us imagine that the football match is over and that the victory dance is in full swing at a nearby marquee or dancehall. In swaggers a man wearing the colours of the losing team. Now while the sporting of colours may be a fine thing at football matches it can be a highly provocative and dangerous business at dances. Only born agitators wantonly do this. Colours are best left at home when the occasion that originally demanded them is no more.

What of the extended use of the badge? A man who wears an Easter Lily on Easter Sunday does so because he wishes to honour the patriot dead but the man who wears it the following week as well is most likely suffering from delusions of patriotic grandeur and should not be provoked or stared at.

Some people have no need for badges. We can tell by their faces the sentiments that lie underneath. We can gauge from their reactions what force impels them. Small things give them away. A man in love, you might say, is a walking badge. They symptoms are written all over him but only for those who are prepared to take a sympathetic look and I am prompted to ask the question should people who fall in love for the first time be made to wear badges? The answer, of course, is yes although I will not go into all the reasons. One or two will suffice. The wearing of a love badge might remind crusty and intolerant old fogies that they too were in love and it might make us all more tolerant of a disorder from which no one at all is immune.

*   *   *   *   *

GARTERS

I am now about to embark upon a treatise trickier than any I have ever tried before. The subject matter is so potentially explosive and fraught with likely dangers that, in this instance, there may be justification for the use of the Shakespearean adage that 'fools rush in where angels fear to tread'. It was Mark Twain who said that 'man is the only animal who blushes and the only animal with reason to blush'. I hope, however, for another blush, the blush of modesty when I disclose the nature of the subject, i. e. the common elastic garter.

The garter has been in wide use from earliest times but did not come into prominence until the year 1351 when the English King Edward III rebuked a number of onlookers when he, the King, reclaimed a garter from the ground. It had been dropped by the Countess of Salisbury after a dance and when he stooped to pick it up he was so irritated by the suggestive laughter of his courtiers that he was quoted as saying: 'Shame on him who thinks ill of it.'

This led to the founding of the Order of the Garter which should clearly indicate that garters were revered even in medieval times.

There is no Irish equivalent of the Order of the Garter. The first reference to garters in Irish history is to be found in the prophecies of the ancient monks of Ballybunion. These particular prophecies, written in Irish might in fact be referring to the youth of today and I am sure that the ancient monks had this very time in mind when they wrote, in reference to the youth of the future, *Beidh siad gan giobal, cleite no bristin*. Translated into English this means: 'They shall be without garter, plume or knickers.'

We must wait and see whether the monks were wholly right or only partly right. The way things are going it's odds on that they weren't too far wrong.

The monks resided on the Virgin Rock off the rugged cliffs of Doon which stand guard over the golden beaches of Ballybunion. Of the Virgin Rock local legend says this: 'A virgin will not be found within an ass's roar of it till all the seas are still and the tides cease to pour.'

All this, however, is getting us nowhere. The subject is garters and I will now endeavour to adhere to them. At the time of writing the only folk wearing garters are hurlers and footballers not to mention the odd old lady who refuses to succumb to tights and still wears pairs of stockings maintained by elastic garters. Referees also wear garters, although many an irate partisan would prefer to see them round their necks rather than their legs.

When I was a gorsoon garters were all the go and I have lost track of the number of times I was sent to neighbourhood emporiums for yards of black and white elastic ranging from an inch in width to a quarter inch. Older ladies and dowdier ladies would wear gibbles or giobals, i. e. garters without elastic or if you like any sort of an old cloth which would hold up a pair of stockings. Gibbles were frowned upon by ladies of fashion and it was also common knowledge that they left deep circular welts around the base of the thigh. The fatter the thigh the deeper the welt. Consequently, a lady who was fond of wearing a bathing costume at opportune times had to be very careful about selecting suitable garters. Wide garters left little or no marking on the thigh whereas a narrow garter often bit into tender flesh and left a red band around this most sensitive of areas. Only two kinds of elastic went into the making of garters in provincial Ireland. White elastic was worn by maids and black elastic was worn only by married women and widows, although if certain widows chose to wear white elastic allowance was always made.

The question which arises here is this. Will there be a return to garters? The answer is, of course, yes. There will be a return to garters when women abandon their slavish habits. The trouble with women is when one wears tights they all wear tights but I say to you, as others have said to me, that garters will be as plentiful in my time and yours as was once the moose on the shores of Lake Huron and the midges that swarm under the bowers near the lakes of Killarney.

Garters also played the part of guardian against incursions above the knee. The garter was the timberline of morality and the Plimsoll Line of security. Can the same be said for tights?

*   *   *   *   *

THE SKIN

How complicated has become the beautification of the female face and body in the past few years. 'Tis a poor dressing table these days that hasn't twenty different items from vanishing cream to nail varnish and from common hand cream to the latest in depilatory devices.

'Removes surplus hair' the label on one of these last announced 'do no apply where abrasions, cuts and scratches appear.' Nearby, however, in a gleaming green bottle shaped like a human heart was written the following: 'Enriches and softens unruly hair; thickens existing hair and brings relief to itchy scalps.'

Maybe you are one of those unfortunate creatures who is afflicted with oily skin. If you are your worries are over because there is a luminous cream which comes in a long jar of satiny texture and which if one is to believe the legend conceived on its exterior EFFECTIVELY ERADICATES THE GREASE AND OIL FROM OVER-ENDOWED SKINS.

Are you plagued by pimples? Please tell me for I have the very thing to remove them painlessly. It is called 'Killpimple' and on its label there is this clearcut warning to pimples of all shapes and sizes 'One dab and you are a pimple less. Dab your pimples away without damage to the natural oils of your skin.'

Maybe you are one of those unfortunates who has rough skin on your feet. If you are and if you are willing to gamble I may have the very thing for you. It is called 'Sweetfeet'. This is what you do: 'Rub a little and allow the skin to absorb same. Remove rough skin gently. Smooth silky skin remains.' I am not having you on. It's all written on the label as plain as a pikestaff for anyone to see.

One of the hazards if you use a cleansing cream frequently is the danger of interference with natural lubrication. Until recently I foolishly believed that anyone who was lubricated was three-quarters drunk or in more even fractions, half-cut. This is not so. Many cleansing creams now contain specially-prepared ingredients (sounds like a fruit-cake) which are guaranteed not to remove, reduce or counterdetract (ideal word) the natural oils of the skin. I call this the height of thoughtfulness.

Would you like to come to terms with dry skin? If you are sincere here is the remedy. It is called 'Aqua Delarosa'. It comes in a yellow bottle with a mauve screwcap. Wouldn't the name alone put the heart crossways on whatever it is knocks the wetness out of our skins and leaves us with dryness?

First of all you shake you bottle of 'Aqua Delarosa' thoroughly and then you pour it on your palm. Apply gently and soothingly to the dry surface over a period of not less than three weeks. This according to the label 'will make dry skin disappear.' I wonder if there was a mixture that would make women disappear how many millions its concocter would make?

Now here's a straight question. Just answer yes or no. Do you want to be 'a girl in a million with a fragrance like the first breath of spring, a lilting, laughing up-to-date girl, vibrant, tingling and exciting'? Take your time. Sit down and ponder well before you answer.

You do? Well here is how you go about it. You go out this instant and invest in a bottle of 'Muguet des Buguet', number nine and you dab it behind your ears and wherever else you think needs a dab of it. Then you sit back and wait until you begin to feel wonderful. Don't thank me. Thank the genius who spent long lonely nights inventing it.

While we're at it here's another. Take your ease as the answer could affect your entire life. Ready? Do you want to tingle from head to toe and feel like seventeen again? All you have to do is fill a bath with hot and cold water and add a dash of 'Bujolay's Bubbly Bathsalts.' As God is my judge, that's all.

I realise I have only skimmed the surface with these few preparations I have paraded before you. Regard them as merely an introduction to a fragrant dreamworld of mystique where there are no corns or cuticles, no bunions, blackheads or warts, where carabuncles and blisters are permanently outlawed and where if a surplus hair were to raise its head it would be the same as signing its death warrant. Regard these simple suggestions of mine as no more than the makings of an overture to the great unwritten symphony of scents, oils and creams beneficial.

Finally, a personal question which you are not obliged to answer. I would not ask it if I did not believe it to be valid and important.

Your elbows? Are they flaked? Are they chapped or are they shiny? You have the night long to answer but remember this. It is your elbows that are in question, not mine.

*   *   *   *   *

MIDDLE-AGED MEN

Middle-aged men, from the first of mankind, have taken unto themselves full rights of pious pontification in every generation right up to this present one. With the immunity that is guaranteed by age and standing they hold forth at length to those under their control. To give them their due it must be said that their pontifications have always been confined to two favourite themes to the almost total exclusion of all others.

These would be in order of merit, the perfidy, villainy and total wantonness of the youth of today and secondly the terrible times we live in.

I remember hearing my own father holding forth when I was a schoolboy. He had just eaten a hearty breakfast and was in the middle of the morning paper. Suddenly he folded the pages the better to concentrate on a particular item of news. He read it out for us. It had to do with the overthrow of a South American government by means of a revolution which claimed the lives of thousands and the lifelong incarceration of thousands more.

'We live,' said he between belches, 'in terrible times.'

What he should have said was this: 'We have always lived in terrible times, we live now in terrible times and, if experience is any guide, we will continue to live in terrible times.'

When dealing with the youth he was never given to oral expression. So awful were the current crop of miscreants and so heinous their crimes that all he could do was shake his head in horror and disbelief as new stories of drunkeness, debauchery and assorted devilment came to hand. If what he heard from another shocked parent was bad in the extreme he would take his pipe from his mouth and make the sign of the cross with the stem. Then and only then would be permit himself one profound yet simple comment.

'Ah,' he would say with a simultaneous shake of the head, 'the youth of today beats all.'

Nothing has changed since the first father expressed disillusionment at the waywardness of his and everybody else's offspring. We may take it then that the two predominant areas for future parental dissemination will be those we have mentioned, i. e. the youth of today and the terrible times we live in.

In my own youth there were famines, plagues, wars, bombings and all the usual suffering that thoughtless men inflict upon each other. There were revolutions and overthrowings of governments. There were religious and sectarian killings and there were assassinations. There were cease-fires and truces and breaches of both but man learned nothing at all in spite of everything.

That is why I have always maintained that life should not be taken too seriously and that even the most cherished ideologies should nearly always be taken with a grain of salt so that men and women might live natural lives and wonder at the beauty of creation rather than conflicting opinions and the carnage created by man.

There are times when I am reminded of my father. I sit reading the paper and I am aghast at the same terrible news. I am on the point of saying to myself that the times we live in are the most terrible of all and I chide myself for repeating age-old inanities.

With regard to the youth of today I must say that allowing for circumstances they are no different to the youth of all the other generations since man first woke up from his sleep wondering about the whereabouts of his son or daughter.

The moral here is that you cannot put an old head on young shoulders no more than you can account for the doings of selfish and heedless men. In short nothing ever really changes and the youth of the day will always be the bane of those who are safely ensconced in middle-age security, who fear for their possessions and their survival and who forget that they were young themselves.

It will always be thus and the statements being made to-day about the youth and the terrible times will be repeated in every generation till Gabriel wipes his lips and trumpets the close of the long game.

As for the past, be certain that it has all been said. If you don't believe me listen to what Shakespeare has to say in *A Winter's Tale*: 'I would there were no age between sixteen and twenty-three or that youth would sleep out the rest for there is nothing in between but getting wenches with child, wronging the ancientry, stealing, fighting.'

Shakespeare surely was attentive to the pontifications of his father. How else could he so accurately convey a middle-aged man's intolerance.

*   *   *   *   *

STREAKING

And as the hare whom hounds and horns pursue,
Pants to the place from whence at first she flew,
He still had hopes, his naked streaking past
Home to return and don his clothes at last.
                    (With apologies to Goldsmith.)

Now, for the want of something better, we will concern ourselves with the anomaly known as Streaking. To streak is to sprint in a public place, dressed only in one's birthday suit, from a specially selected base, over an appointed course having as its terminus the original starting place.

I am aware of no other definition of Streaking and if there is another I will gladly stand corrected provided it is better than the one submitted by me now with due respect to lexicologists everywhere. The root cause of present-day streaking is to be found in the vast uncharted cosmos which is human energy. In simple terms your Streaker is a man or woman over-endowed with that quality known as taspy or jizz.

Streaking, of course, has been part and parcel of man's makeup since the trousers were invented. Down the ages men have streaked for different reasons and we shall deal with these presently as soon as we have finished with today's phenomenon.

The main reason, as already indicated, for the most recent outbreak of Streaking, is excess energy. The supplementary reasons are wagering, the impressing of girls and strong drink. Let us now look to other generations in an effort to obtain a comprehensive picture of this much-maligned outdoor activity.

I was a wise old gentleman of five when I encountered my first Streaker. My mother and myself were on our way from eight o'clock Mass of a bitter mid-March morning when out of the hail-ridden gloom there appeared the figure of a man, naked from head to toe without so much as a hat on his head. He passed us by like a flash with a crazed look in his bloodshot eyes. My mother crossed herself and we made haste.

I stole a quick look round but the man was nowhere to be seen, having suddenly vanished into thin air. Over the years I frequently saw the same gentleman streaking over the same course at approximately the same time.

We will call him Flash McNab which is not his real name but is like enough to it and is fashioned purely to suit our purpose. Flash McNab was neither an exhibitionist nor a sex maniac. Whenever the poor fellow arrived home drunk on a Saturday night his puritanical mother would hide his hat, clothes and shoes, his workaday clothes and any other garments in his possession. This was to discourage further alcoholic forays.

In the morning Flash would wake with a sick head but without clothes or money. His one desire was for strong drink. So great was this desire that he would streak naked over the seventy exposed yards of roadway to the nearest public house. The door of this most accommodating hostelry was never locked. Here he would consume the necessary medicaments and when the sickness was removed he would borrow an overcoat from the proprietor for the return journey.

When his mother died he abandoned his practice of nude sprinting and married a neighbourhood spinster who always kept a drop in the house lest he be tempted to return to his former habits. In my youth there were many Streakers of the Flash McNab variety. The hiding of a man's apparel was considered as good and as legitimate a way as any to keep him away from the booze. Let us now press on and look at

82

another form of streaking.

There is a romantic type of elderly gentleman who never loses the mind of women. His desire for females is as potent during the final stages of senility as it was when he first became conscious of the opposite sex.

In country places this is facetiously called the heat-before-death although I have heard less complimentary appellations. Potent, however, as this late desire is there can be no hope of a matching physical performance and when these old gentlemen kick off their clothes to cavort in public places we would do well to remember that this is Streaking of a purely symbolic nature or, if you like, the ultimate tribute to former prowess.

Country folk are most tolerant of this sort of Streaking and many good-humouredly excuse such antics on the grounds that they are nothing more and nothing less than bullocks' notions, i. e., the futile notions entertained by bullocks when they encounter willing cows and heifers.

So we have shown that there is more to this business of Streaking than appears on the surface. This current rash of streaking, as I have pointed out, seems to be the prerogative of young people and before we start to criticise it we should think on what the old woman said when the bonham jumped out of the rail.

'Youth,' said she, 'must have its fling.'

*   *   *   *   *

SNORING

Snoring is on the decline.

The greater, long-nosed, pot-bellied snorer is now the exception rather than the rule.

It was a wise man who said: 'Laugh and the world laughs with you; snore and you sleep alone', because a snorer is not loved. He may be loved while he is up and about but after the first fitful snort he may find himself alone on his couch, deserted by his spouse who has found sanctuary in the beds of her offspring. Even then she may not be safe for a snore with a snarl in it has insidious powers of penetration. Only a solid stone wall is proof against its rolling pitches.

Man is the noisiest of sleepers. No animal would dare sound off from such an unprotected position but then man is surrounded by walls and therefore safe from his enemies. It may be suggested that when man slept out-of-doors he developed the snore to frighten off his enemies while he slept. This is untrue. A hungry lion or tiger is not put off by a snore. In fact he is attracted by it and the more experienced denizens often spend an enjoyable hour or two guessing the proportions of the snorer. They can tell from the snorts, snarls and rumbles whether the victim is meaty or bony. A rumbling snore predicts prime condition whereas a reedy, rattling snore suggests a candidate for the boneyard, not that a hunting man-eater's too particular but there is every reason to believe that he will eat the fat snorer first.

With regard to snoring, I would like to kill a widely-believed and universally popular myth. We are told in fairy tales of giants whose snores uprooted trees and laid hills as flat as pancakes. The sound of the snores could be heard in the four corners of the kingdom and, remember, there were kingdoms in those days, not like now. At the outset let me say that I deny neither the giants nor the snores but I question the fact that giants snored loudly and, indeed, doubt very much if they snored at all. I suspect, and other eminent authorities agree with me, that the authors of these magnificent snores were medium-sized ordinary men, in appearance not unlike to the average suburban householder of today. In those days there were wolves and bears prowling about constantly so that loud snoring was developed principally as a defensive weapon. So, when you hear a loud snorer today, the blame lies not with him but with ancestors who held the night terrors at bay with the awful intensity of their snoring.

Few people, if any, can be persuaded to share a bed with a known snorer. The youngest member of the household is, of course, always available, not from sympathy, oddly enough, but rather from curiosity. I hesitate to call him an apprentice but the desire to emulate is strong. However if he is studied closely he will be seen to watch the snorer silently for long periods so that it is probable that the prime motivator was curiosity. There is always the danger, however, that he will attempt to imitate the sounds made by the snorer or that he will interfere with the snorer. Interference invariably results in a series of snorts, grunts and snarls of such volume and variety that the whole household is alerted and further sleep is out of the question.

I have often been asked if I knew of a good cure for snoring. Since I do not look upon snoring as a malady, I hesitated to suggest an antidote. I find snoring—distant snoring, naturally—soothing and consoling. As a child I was enraptured by distant snoring and it brought happiness in the night's darkest hours. It assured one that there was somebody else in the world and while snoring continued there was a guarantee that a small child would not wake up to find himself forsaken. Distant dogs barking or crying curlew do not bring the same solace. A snore is an assurance that one is with one's own kind and it shows that there is at least one man, if one is to judge by the audacity of his snoring, who holds nothing but contempt for the terrors of the night.

One must remember, nevertheless, that the world is full of people who cannot sleep while somebody in the house is snoring. I know a woman who tape-recorded her husband's snoring and played it back to him. To this day he refuses to believe that the noise was made by him and she has no way of convincing him.

Another woman I know tried stuffing her husband's nose with cotton wool. How naive can a person be? The wool was immediately discharged from the muscular nostrils with the power and sound of a well-oiled double barrell gun. There followed an assertive snort and the snoring was taken up where it was left off the night before.

Few people know that there is a positive cure for snoring and I see no reason why it should not be divulged. The cure, of course, is porter. It is not true to say that porter will cure almost anything but taken in the right doses it will cure all except chronic snoring, since it is commonly known that a man with porter in his hold sleeps with his mouth open.

*   *   *   *   *

A TALE OF TWO SAUSAGES

I was in digs once upon a time with a man who loved sausages.

Perhaps I shouldn't have said *loved* but I am sure you know what I mean. He was inordinately found of sausages with a preference for peppery dicks which are eight to the pound and were possibly the most melodious of all sausages while frying. There were other sausages twenty-four to the pound and sixteen to the pound and there were cocktail sausages which, if I may be permitted to quote, 'He could hould atin' from one end of the year to the other.' He never entered for sausage-eating championships. He was no glutton either. All he wanted was his fill of sausages. Sometimes he was not above practising deception if he could not fill his quota. The third chap in digs was a bald-headed cadaverous-looking schoolmaster from Brecknock in south Wales. Despite his appearance he was a jovial fellow, a useful man in a publichouse, although surprisingly enough he had no interest in Rugby football. He backed horses too, unsuccessfully if memory serves me correctly but his forte was ring-throwing and I once saw him lay eight in a row while mildly intoxicated.

But where was I?

Yes, as I say, he was an agreeable fellow and the three of us got along well together until the landlady disappeared unexpectedly one morning, without prior notice to her husband, to take up residence with another gentleman.

It was the practice of the landlady, before she chose the second mate, to give us, on Saturday evenings, a sizeable supper of the mixed-grill variety. There would be chips and peas, a chop, a bit of liver, a cube of pudding and always two composite sausages of the eight to the pound class. These were fondly called Peppery Dicks and in case you do not know I feel constrained to inform you that only sausages that run eight to the pound may be legitimately dubbed Peppery Dicks.

On this particular Saturday evening we sat at table in the dining room, a large cheerful room with an endearing bay window flimsily curtained so that one could see into the street beyond without being noticed from the outside.

At the head of the table sat the landlord, a morose man of few words, who once had collapsed at work when told that the tea-boiler had burst. Perhaps if he was given more to conversation the wife might never have left him. Truth to tell, I never heard the couple argue or fight. Maybe they did not consider it worth their while. Believe me, many of these relaxed taken-for-granted liaisons can be of short duration.

Finally the supper arrived with all the usual ingredients. There was little conversation since the landlord seemed to frown on it. I will say this for him. He had a phobia about peas. 'Eat your peas, lads,' he would say if any of us were remiss in the matter of demolishing them. He followed this by telling us that peas were good for us. He said no more, and he never told us why they were good for us. One could hardly doubt him because of the sincere manner in which he stressed his sentiments. However, as I say, our plates were now before us and after a few peremptory harrumphs we were soon under starter's orders and making the most of the fare.

Here, however, the plot thickens and you will be advised to take note of what I am about to say as it may be of some assistance to you should you ever be forced into digs.

Our friend who loved sausages, naturally enough, started with the sausages. He then asked me to swap my sausages for his piece of liver, which I did, not because I dislike sausages but it would be fair to say that I am somewhat indifferent to them. Now the Welshman was that sort of eater who begins with the chop, working his way patiently through chips, liver and pudding and concluding with the sausages. He had reached the stage of the meal where only the two sausages and one chip remained on his plate. At this stage he was being watched curiously by the sausage-lover. Casually he downed the chip, then readjusting himself in the chair he prepared to tackle the sausages.

'Why, bless my soul!' said the sausage-lover.

'What is it?' we asked.

'Why, I could have sworn,' he said, and he pointed to the big window, 'that I saw Blodwyn Evans of Brecknock passing just now.'

The Welshman jumped to his feet immediately and rushed to the window which he opened, the better to see out into the street. While his back was turned the sausage-lover slipped the two sausages off his plate and had them fully swallowed before the Welshman had time to turn around. The Welshman look at his empty plate and said nothing. The landlord was genuinely shocked. It was an act utterly beyond his comprehension. For once he left his peas unfinished and sat transfixed to his chair.

'You'll have to excuse me,' said the sausage-lover, 'I have to dash off!'

With that he rose as if nothing had happened, picked his teeth dreamily with a broken match-stick and departed the scene without further ado.

*   *   *   *   *

A STRANGE ENCOUNTER

The other evening I found myself on top of a hill miles from anywhere. Suddenly the sky darkened and without announcement a horde of hard-hitting hailstones bore down upon me.

I did what any reasonable man would do under the circumstances. I bade farewell to my immediate surroundings and fled to where a cluster of leafless bushes offered protection of a sort. I crouched as low as I could, proferring as little of myself as possible to the now furious flight of hail. It is astonishing how innocuous a hailstone looks when its journey is done and it rests with millions of fellows along the exposed margin of a roadway.

Misfortune, we are told, brings strange bedfellows and shortly after I had taken refuge I was joined, under the hedge, by a gaunt bearded man whom I had noticed earlier making social calls to farmers' houses along my route. He was better at crouching that I was. He was also, despite the oddity and number of his garments, better dressed for the occasion. I saluted him respectively and while he glanced at me curiously he did not bother to acknowledge my greeting.

'Sudden change!' I said, hoping he would at least respond in some way by word or sign. The hail passed quickly enough but was followed by a sizzling unrelenting rain which found its way through the hedge and settled upon various parts of our persons.

In the middle of all this, while I exhibited discomfort by twisting and turning myself into all shapes and sizes, the bearded man sat calmly and obliviously on his haunches and proceeded to produce a number of unusual articles from his pockets. These consisted of four cold boiled potatoes, a handkerchief which contained a few chunks of fat boiled bacon and, finally, a porter bottle full of milk. I gathered there were the fruits of his house-calls. He laid out the articles lovingly on his lap and proceeded to make an enjoyable meal. He ate is if he were alone in the world. He did not invite me to join him. I wouldn't if he had but it would have been mannerly of him if he did. He had a method of eating with which I was not familiar in that he rejected nothing. I could have sworn there were some small bones in the bacon and I'm certain I heard these being crushed by his gigantic yellow teeth. I was tempted to ask him if this was so but he was so absorbed in his task that I decided not to burden him with any query at the time. He produced a small mustard canister which contained a mixture of salt and mustard. He spiced his food from time to time with pinches of mixture, belched outrageously but with apparent satisfaction and no apology.

You are a surly type of fellow, I said, not to him but to myself, and what's more, your manners are a disgrace. He looked at me briefly but chillingly as if he could read my mind. He then proceeded to devour the remains of the meal. Finally he belched once more, a complimentary belch more musical than its predecessors. It was a belch as expressive as the most skilfully embroidered compliment.

He wiped his hands on the wet grass and dried them on the insides of his garments. He uncorked the milk bottle and took a small swallow. He then produced a smaller bottle which, when he uncorked it smelled suspiciously like paraffin oil, or lamp-oil as we call it in country places. He added half the lamp-oil to the milk and then, bracing himself, he swallowed the lot. He grinned first, then he screwed up his wrinkled bearded face into a seraphic smile. He grinned again as the liquid made itself felt in his innards. Then his whole body shook with a single great spasm and I thought his lights were about to go out. He recovered quickly and proceeded to rearrange his chattles. This he did as if the job were a delight. He unwound the ropes or rags which held his clothes together and then set about tying them together again. He was expert at this.

He took off his boots and withdrew several layers of wet cardboard and paper. These he replaced with fresh layers which he produced from inside his shirt. He tied the boots and stood erect. There was a regality about him even when he stooped to pick up his coat. I could have sworn that there was contempt in his face when our eyes met. I rose quickly since the rain had stopped.

'Good luck now!' I said to him but to this he made no reply. I hurried down the hill only to find that he was by my side matching my long steps with ease. At the cross-roads we parted. He went away without a word and on reflection I was forced to concede that he was the best of companions. He had demanded nothing. I had intruded on his thoughts and privacy yet so great was his patience and experience of people like me that he had not rebuffed me by a single word or deed.

*   *   *   *   *

BUCKET HANDLES

I was entering a hostelry in Killarney when I was approached by a man who accused me of never having written about bucket handles.

'Buckets you have,' he said, 'and chamber-pots you have, garters you have and half-doors you have but bucket handles never.' I admitted to the charge and pointed out that my accuser had never written about bucket handles either.

'It's not my job,' he said, 'it's yours.' With that he left me. I do not know the man nor do I know where he hailed from but let us, in the interests of open-mindedness, take up the challenge as it were and have a gander at this business of bucket handles. In the first place there are as many types of handles as there are types of buckets so that we must not presume that the most celebrated of all buckets, i. e. the old wooden bucket had an old wooden handle for the good reason that enamel buckets do not have enamel handles so that we are are without guidelines of any kind at the outset.

Let us, therefore, take a particular bucket. We have enamel, steel, wooden, tin and galvanised. Let us take your common or garden galvanised bucket for no other reason than it is the most common of all buckets and also because it has a galvanised handle. This, at least, is consistency of a kind and we are now better girded for our investigation having, so to speak, a recognisable subject, to wit, the galvanised handle of a galvanised bucket.

It is an object which is not without artistry. Delicately shaped like a sickle and with curls at both ends it is highly musical in the best metallic sense. It has a pleasant, silvery appearance and while its intrinsic worth is negligible it can be used in a hundred different ways as any handy man will tell you. It is a thing of great endurance and I know of no instance where the galvanised bucket has outlived the galvanised handle.

It is without peer in the matter of tethering goats, asses, mules and small ponies and I have have seen a pair of galvanised handles from modestly-proportioned parent-buckets used as hinges on a gate which was created from an iron bedstead. This composition of discards cost not a single penny and yet it served the purpose of an article which could cost a small farmer a considerable sum of money.

I also recall an elderly whitewasher who, in my childhood, used to whitewash our backyard. He had his own ladder and tools of the trade. These latter consisted of a large galvanised bucket, two brushes, one wide as a handlebar moustache for the rough work and the other purposely narrow as a Chinese pigtail for the whitening of niches, cracks, holes and assorted cicitraces. In addition to these expected paraphernalia there was also a galvanised bucket handle. This was used only when the whitewasher was operating from the higher rungs of the ladder. It served to attach the whitewash bucket to the most convenient rung. Few whitewashers can whitewash and hold on to a full bucket at the same time while also endeavouring to manoeuvre at the top of an unsteady leadder.

What the whitewasher did was elevate the bucket handle which was attached to the bucket and to place the extra or spare bucket handle underneath it. He then sqeezed both ends of the spare in an arc over the chosen rung so that the bucket hung safely. Whenever he climbed higher all the whitewasher had to do was pull the ends of the spare handle apart and re-attach the bucket in the elementary manner aforementioned.

Let it be carefully recorded, however, that the spare bucket handle did not complete its services with this action alone. No indeed for when the whitewasher returned to *terra firma* for the purpose of mixing more whitewash he used the spare bucket handle for stirring the lime which made the whitewash. Not only this but when the job of whitewashing was complete the spare handle was rapped smartly against the sides of the bucket to disengage loose flakes and foreign bodies which attached themselves to the bucket during the day's whitewashing.

Your galvanised handle has no peer when it came to lifting the covers of roasting-hot skillets and bastable ovens. All one had to do was insert the handle under the little handle which was attached to the lid and place the cover to one side of the hearth while the contents of the utensil in use were examined to see if they were properly cooked or a few more minutes were required to finish off the job.

Now because of space restrictions I will have to draw to a close but not before I make a few final, meaningful observations. As a back-scratcher your galvanised bucket handle is to be seen at its best. Its natural curvature assists the scratcher in a way that few other implements can and if it served no other purpose but this it would occupy a valuable place in the history of therapeutics.

Lastly if one should happen to be locked out at night after a dance or carousel there is nothing more effective than the handle in question. It will not break a window if thrown gently in that direction but when it strikes the pane the resultant noise is far more irritating and lasting than if the window were smashed in the first place. I hope that in making these few observations regarding bucket handles we will have answered our friend in Killarney and also show that there is no subject under the sun about which a decent treatise cannot be written.

LETTERS OF A SUCCESSFUL T.D.

This bestseller takes a humourous peep at the correspondence of an Irish parliamentary deputy. Keane's eyes have fastened on the human weaknesses of a man who secured power through the ballot box, and uses it to ensure the comfort of his family and friends.

LETTERS OF AN IRISH PARISH PRIEST

There is a riot of laughter in every page and its theme is the correspondence between a country parish priest and his nephew who is studying to be a priest. Father O'Mora has been referred to by one of his parishioners as one who 'is suffering from an overdose of racial memory aggravated by religious bigotry.' John B. Keane's humour is neatly pointed, racy of the soil and never forced. This book gives a picture of a way of life which though in great part is vanishing is still familiar to many of our countrymen who still believe 'that priests could turn them into goats.' It brings out all the humour and pathos of Irish life. It is hilariously funny and will entertain and amuse everyone.

LETTERS OF A LOVE-HUNGRY FARMER

John B. Keane has introduced a new word into the English language — *chastitute*. This is the story of a chastitute, i.e. a man who has never lain down with a woman for reasons which are fully disclosed within this book. It is the tale of a lonely man who will not humble himself to achieve his heart's desire, whose need for female companionship whines and whimpers throughout. Here are the hilarious sex escapades of John Bosco McLane culminating finally in one dreadful deed.